www.moshimonsters.com

SUNBIRD
PENGUIN

Published by Ladybird Books Ltd 2012
A Penguin Company
Penguin Books Ltd, 80 Strand, London, WC2R 0RL, UK
Penguin Group (USA) Inc., 375 Hudson Street, New York 10014, USA
Penguin Books Australia Ltd, Camberwell Road, Camberwell, Victoria 3124,
Australia (A division of Pearson Australia Group Pty Ltd)
Canada, India, New Zealand, South Africa

Written by Steve Cleverley
Illustrations by Vincent Bechet, Ross McCaughey and Trevor White
Sunbird is a trademark of Ladybird Books Ltd

www.ladybird.com

ISBN: 978-1-40939-095-4
003 - 10 9 8 7 6 5 4 3
Printed in Slovakia

Moshi monsters™

THE ULTIMATE MOSHLINGS COLLECTOR'S GUIDE

Contents

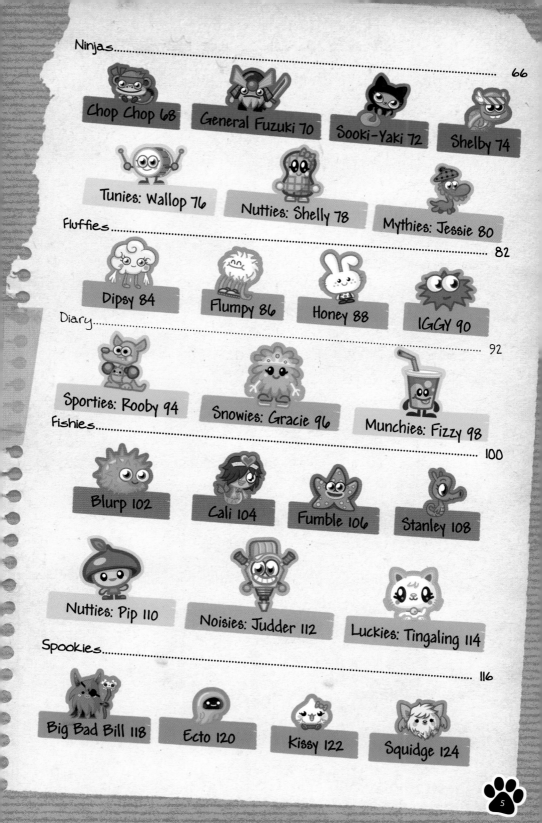

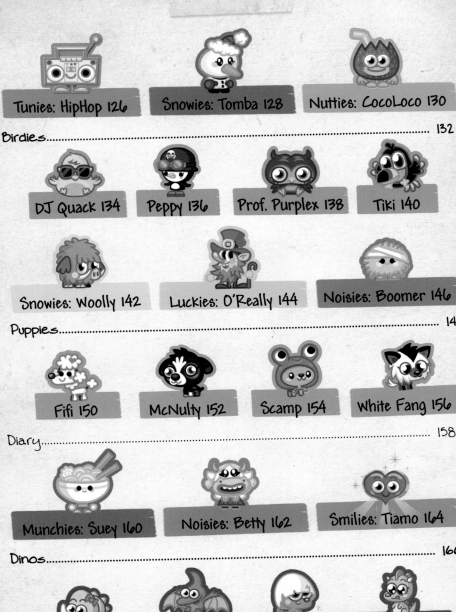

Greetings, Fellow Moshling Hunters!

Buster Bumblechops, Moshling expert extraordinaire at your service.

If you're looking for Moshlings, then you've come to the right place. This handy field guide is jam-packed with everything you need to know about the teeny-weeny critters. And I should know, because it was written by yours truly. Yep, that's me!

I've always said that collecting Moshlings is trickier than untangling pretzels wearing boxing gloves dipped in treacle. Thankfully your ol' pal Buster is an expert (at collecting Moshlings, not untangling pretzels).

Yours truly

Thing is, just lately I've been on so many expeditions and discovered so many new Moshlings it's hard to keep track.
It's even harder with my assistant Snuffy Hookums still missing. And paperwork has never been my thing (unless you're talking about making paper planes or silly Hoodoo masks).

Buster aged 3 1/4

But I want to keep y'all bang up to date so I've gathered together a whole heap of my latest finds and thrown them

8

across the following pages. Not literally - that would be messy. Some of these Moshlings are so new they could even be extra-special one-offs. Even I don't know what sets they belong to. Any ideas? Only time will tell but I'll keep you posted, promise. Happy huntin'!

As you can tell, Moshling hunting is not all fun and games. Well, okay, it is. But it takes a special kind of monster to tame these itty-bitty beasties. Think you can handle it?

Keep this book with you at all times, and at least you'll know what to expect next time you come face-to-face with Ecto the Fancy Banshee or O'Really the Unlucky Larrikin!

Happy huntin'!

Buster Bumblechops

Finding Fishies in Potion Ocean . . .

Buster Bumblechops
The Ultimate Moshling Collector

Contact me at:
buster@moshimonsters.com

I'm Gonna Get Ya, IGGY!

My first traps weren't
always very successful . . .

Where is that Gingersnap?

Collecting Moshlings

Howdy doody, eager beavers! Are you ready to start nabbin' yourselves a few Moshlings? Good, 'cos when it comes to roundin' up the playful little scamps, your old pal Buster is an expert.

Of course, some of my rootin' tootin' trapping techniques are far too risky for all you whippersnappers out there. And I wouldn't want you vanishing into thin air like my poor ol' great uncle! Or even Snuffy!

So, how do you get your mitts on a Moshling without risking your neck? All you need to get started are seeds! They're the sure-fire way to attract the teeny-weeny critters. So quit scratching your noodle and check out my seed-tastic tips. They're sure to grow on you!

STAR BLOSSOM

SNAP APPLE

As any budding collector knows, Moshlings are attracted to flowers — and seeds make flowers. Just hightail it over to

www.moshimonsters.com

and buy yourself some seeds. If you're lucky enough to be a Moshi Member you can skedaddle on over to The Port area and buy extra-special seeds like Crazy Daisies and Snap Apples to attract rarer Moshlings.

HOT SILLY PEPPERS

MOON ORCHID

In total there are eight weird and wonderful seed varieties. Plant them in the three plots in your garden and watch 'em grow. Sounds easy, huh? Well, sometimes it is, but different blooms attract different Moshlings, so you need to get your combinations just right. You dig?

LOVE BERRIES

DRAGON FRUIT

MAGIC BEANS

CRAZY DAISY

If you're looking to snag something Ultra Rare, you'll need to make sure your flowers are the right colour, too. Hot diggity, talk about fussy! If you don't get lucky straight away, relax. A birdie boffin called the Cluekoo will swoop in with a few helpful hints. Next time you crack a combination, why not share it with your friends?

Of course, not all Moshling collecting is about keeping your garden growing! There are many ways to track down the little munchkins, including helping out the Super Moshis over at the Volcano, so keep your eyes peeled at all times. You never know when you might have the opportunity to add to your collection! I might be a Moshling collector extraordinaire, but even I'm surprised at where they turn up sometimes . . . There's space at the back of my guide to add your own notes on where you've come across them.

Keeping Your Moshlings

Collecting Moshlings isn't quite as easy-peasy-gooberry-squeezy as ol' Buster makes it look. But once you get the hang of it you'll be swamped with little pets, so you'll need somewhere to keep 'em.

After all, who wants squillions of kooky characters scurrying, fluttering and waddling around their crib? Exactly! And I wouldn't recommend stuffing them in your pockets or keeping them under your hat. That's why the Moshling Zoo is so cool.

Ideal for serious collectors, you can keep as many Moshlings as you like in here. Each time you complete a set of four, your Moshlings' pen gets a funky makeover. The lucky critters even get their very own themed houses to hang out in. Mmm, home sweet home! Once they're there, don't you go forgetting about them! They can be grubby little mites so you'll need to make sure you keep them clean and cared for!

ZOO

14

Talking of home, if you're a Moshi Member, you can keep up to six Moshlings in your room at any time. Simply move them between your zoo and house by clicking on the zoo signpost. Switcheroodle-doo! You can even set your Moshlings free if they don't tickle your pickle.

Party time at the ranch!

By now you're probably wondering where I stash all the Moshlings I've collected over the years. No, I don't keep them in my tent. I don't even send them to a zoo or put them in the backyard at Bumblechops Manor.

Truth is, they are free to wander around my secret Moshling ranch, a supersize sanctuary hidden right next to . . . oops, well, slap my head and call me silly! I almost forgot it's a secret. Search all you like, you'll never find it. And believe me, many of my rivals have tried!

Moshling Ranch
17 Secret Street,
Moshi World

Beasties

With a name like Beasties, you would be forgiven for thinking these Moshlings were wild and ferocious. Thankfully most of 'em are harmless, though I've had a few tricksy run-ins with them in my time. Jeepers will even let you tickle its tummy if you hand over a few cans of swoonafish.

Even Ultra Rare Fiery Frazzledragons can be kept as pets — so long as they don't get hiccups and burn the house down. Perhaps it would be best to kick-start your Beastie collection with a Sneezing Panda. These snuffly channel surfers are happy to go anywhere there's a big screen and remote control.

Or maybe you should plant some seeds for a Snoring Hicko. They are pretty easy to attract and spend most of their time catching Zs. But so would you if you gulped lazy daisy moonshine all day.

Most Moshlingologists believe Beasties are direct descendants of Sillysauruses, which means they are slightly related to Dinos. But don't tell them that. Who wants a snarly ol' lizard for a granddaddy?

Oh yes, I almost forgot. All Beasties can recite the alphabet backwards.

Ynnuf, huh!

zyxwvuts rqponmlk jihgfedcba

To claim your exclusive virtual gift, go to the sign-in page of **MOSHIMONSTERS.COM** and enter the first word in the personality section on page 120. Your surprise free gift will appear in your treasure chest!

Burnie
the Fiery Frazzledragon

Personality: combustible, dangerous, cheeky

Too hot to handle!

ULTRA RARE

Burnie

Flaming hiccups!

Other Beasties:

Humphrey the Snoring Hickopotumus	✓
Jeepers the Snuggly Tiger Cub	✓
ShiShi the Sneezing Panda	✓

If you can stand the heat, you might find a few fiery frazzledragons fluttering around Mount CharChar, on the volcanic island of Emberooze.

These cheeky flying beasties get into all kinds of sizzly mayhem, especially if they've been guzzling gasoline. It's their favourite drink but it gives them terrible flaming hiccups. Stand back or you might get toasted! (I've been lightly barbecued a few times, but nothing too serious.) Some time ago I discovered ancient scribblings in a cave by the Lava Lakes. My translator, Dr Unwin Babble, thinks they prove Frazzledragons were once employed by Super Moshis to heat up cauldrons of dew stew and chargrill silly sausages.

Hiccup!

Paw print

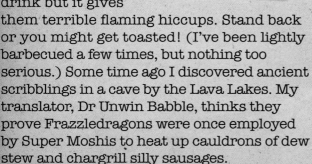

Habitat

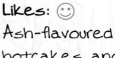

Likes: ☺
Ash-flavoured hotcakes and the Moshi MonStars' new single.

Dislikes: ☹
Fire extinguishers and round tables.

Code to catch Burnie:

SNAP APPLE **RED** + SNAP APPLE **RED** + CRAZY DAISY **BLUE**

Humphrey

the Snoring Hickopotumus

Personality: happy-go-lucky, snoozy, bumpkinly

Yee-hah! Quit lollygagging around and say howdy to the good ol' Moshlings that love digging, sowing, milking and mowing. If they're not busy working the ranch, Snoring Hickos enjoy grabbing forty winks under the shade of a wacky windmill. Trouble is, forty winks often turns into forty hours and that's a mighty long time when you're supposed to be mixing lazy daisy moonshine.

I've been lucky enough to visit several Hicko ranches, and nothing beats watching the sun go down after a rollicking barn dance and a few slugs of Hicko firewater.

'Urp!

Habitat

Snoring Hickos live and work on the ranches scattered across Skedaddle Prairie down in Whoop 'n' Holler Valley.

Likes: ☺
Pickin' the banjo and chewing enchanted corn.

Dislikes: ☹
Concrete and the smell of manure in the morning.

Awake, for once!

Catching some ZZZZZZZZs

Humphrey

Code to catch Humphrey:

CRAZY DAISY **ANY** + HOT SILLY PEPPERS **ANY** + MAGIC BEANS **ANY**

Jeepers #073
the Snuggly Tiger Cub

Personality: bashful, soppy, cuddly

RARE

Jeepers

Oops, I pressed 'zoom'!

Pesky critter got its claws on my notes!

Code to catch Jeepers:

LOVE BERRIES

ANY

+

SNAP APPLE

BLUE

+

CRAZY DAISY

RED

These adorable Moshlings really have earned their stripes. That's because they spend ages painting them on using inka-inka juice, squeezed from rare thumpkin seeds. Sadly the jungle is green, not yellow and stripy, so an expert like me has no problem spotting them.

I once disguised myself as a Snuggly to infiltrate their tribe. Sadly it rained and the paint washed off, leaving me looking very silly, licking my paws and scratching for fleas. When they're not slopping hopeless camouflage around, Snuggly Tiger Cubs love sharpening their claws and licking old swoonafish cans.

Even though their camouflage is useless, it's pretty difficult for a normal monster to spot a Snuggly Tiger Cub because they seldom stray beyond the lush foliage of the Barmy Swami Jungle.

Habitat

Other Beasties:

Paw print

Likes: ☺
Glam rock and having their tummies scratched.

Dislikes: ☹
Water pistols and flea collars.

ShiShi
the Sneezing Panda

Personality: friendly, brainy, snoozy

ShiShi ♥

ULTRA RARE

Code to catch ShiShi:

DRAGON FRUIT		HOT SILLY PEPPERS		CRAZY DAISY
	+		+	
RED		**YELLOW**		**BLACK**

Originally from Gogglebox Gulch, these snuffly channel surfers will live anywhere as long as there is a big screen, comfy chair and remote control.

Habitat

Aah-choo! These eyelash-fluttering Moshlings are obsessed with watching Monstrovision, but it makes them sneeze. Lots. My research suggests they might be allergic to all those itty-bitty pixels. Or maybe it's the wamwoo shoots they scoff by the bucket-load. I'm not really sure because I've never had a proper conversation with one. I've tried, but when they're not glued to the screen, Sneezing Pandas are usually fiddling with magical eye drops or scrunching up extra-soft tissues. Next time I spot one, I might just switch off whatever it is they are watching and observe what happens.

Likes: ☺
Channel-hopping and extra-soft tissues.

Dislikes: ☹
Pepper and 'We interrupt this programme!' newsflashes.

Diary

When it comes to jotting down stories about rounding up Beasties, I could scribble away for ages. So I will!

After all, they are such a mixed bunch: from Humphrey and ShiShi to Burnie and Jeepers. And tracking them down never fails to lead to a rip-roaring adventure.

The first Beastie I ever came across was Burnie. I spotted the flame-spewing fella through the high-powered moshiscope aboard my research ship, *Windigo II*, whilst circling the volcanic island of Emberooze.

It was flip-flapping around Mount CharChar collecting lava lumps. But I couldn't get too close 'cos that place is hotter than a bear's backside in a pepper patch.

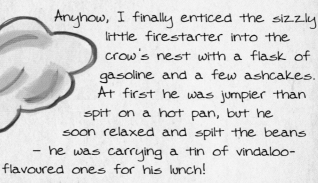

Anyhow, I finally enticed the sizzly little firestarter into the crow's nest with a flask of gasoline and a few ashcakes. At first he was jumpier than spit on a hot pan, but he soon relaxed and spilt the beans – he was carrying a tin of vindaloo-flavoured ones for his lunch!

Over a tongue-scorching snack, he told me all about his fellow Beastie Moshlings. Me? I couldn't do much yakking because the beans were burning my mouth and everything I thaid thounded really thilly!

Worst of all, when I tried to trap him in my net he let out an almighty burp and set fire to my sails. Vwoomp! Thankfully, I was rescued from the blaze by a gaggle of Valley Mermaids riding Songful Seahorses, just as my beloved boat slipped beneath the waves.

Phew-ee!

From that day on I vowed to beware of Beasties, even the ones that can't breathe fire. And it's a good thing I did because I almost came a cropper thanks to a cub called Jeepers and a Hicko by the name of Humphrey . . . but that's a whole 'nuther story!

PS: According to my Fishie friends, the *Windigo II* is still in one piece at the bottom of Potion Ocean! Maybe y'all can salvage some equipment for me next time you're in the area? Thanks!

Zack Binspin
the Moptop Tweenybop
107

Zack Binspin has dreamt of being
a famous singer ever since he saw
Screech McPiehole yelling on *Top
of the Mops*. And now, thanks to his
high-trousered mentor, Simon Growl, that
dream is finally a reality. Zack used to sing backing vocals
for one of Monstro City's biggest bin-bound singers but
solo gooperstardom beckoned the second he
was signed by HighPants Productions.
I'm too old to get caught up in all this
Binspinmania but I have to admit
this Moptop Tweenybop writes
some real toe-tappers. I
might even take his CD
on my next expedition.

Zack's idol

Likes: ☺
Simon Growl and
fishbone combs.

Dislikes: ☹
Rival bin-bound pop
stars and clumsy
Glumps.

ULTRA RARE

ZACK

Zack Binspin

Roarshall

Habitat

Zack comes from Brashcan Alley but hangs out at the Sandy Drain Hotel these days.

Roxy
the Precious Prism

Personality: priceless, fastidious, fragile

Roxy

How to catch Roxy:
This sparkling secret Moshling can only be caught by the most clued-up collectors. Email buster@moshimonsters.com to find out how to add her to your collection!

SECRET You've got to be quick to catch Roxy!

30

Deep beneath the Twinkly-Dink mines of Kaleido Island lies a rich seam of powerful Rox. But Precious Prisms don't hang out down there. It's far too obvious! Plus they might bump into ol' Buster diggin' for sparkly stuff. These secret Moshlings are so priceless they're scared to lay a finger on anything (including themselves!) in case they leave smudges. That's why they wear silly white gloves 24/7. But so would you, if you were made of 100% pure Rox. The only way to catch 'em is to get diggin'. Handle with care; they often shatter into squillions of pieces.

Zzing!

Sparkling in the sunshine

Likes: ☺
Vinegar baths and buffing machines.

Dislikes: ☹
Magpies and fingerprints.

I once spotted a Priceless Prism during the Great Rox Rush of Eleventy Seven, but I can't remember where.

Drat!

Pocito
the Mini Mangler

111

Personality: tenacious, secretive, athletic

Tremendously strong and super elasticky, Mini Manglers are the mysterious masked Moshlings who can't stop wrestling. If you find one practising the latest eye-watering moves do not disturb or you might find yourself in a spinning headlock. I recently asked a Mini Mangler to remove its mask for a photo – bad idea as it proceeded to perform a body avalanche on my camera before putting me in a short-arm scissorlock. I couldn't tie my shoelaces for a week! The Mini Mangler thought it was hilarious and celebrated by rubbing a full-nelson fajita in my face.

Yuck!

Habitat

In the Atomic Slambuster, a secret training camp near the giant haystacks of El Astico Ranch.

Likes: ☺
Nachos and talcum powder.

Dislikes: ☹
Referees and biting.

Recipe for Fried
Oobla Doobla fajitas:

Begin by frying Oobla Doobla in
coconut shells, then mix in two
tablespoons of Silly Chili and

ULTRA
RARE

Pocito

33

Ponies

Saddle up and say howdy to the Ponies, horsey Moshlings with a rich history here in the world of Moshi. Before the invention of the wheel these four-legged little thingummies were often ridden by monsters.

Course, they were far too titchy for big ol' Furis and Katsumas, so as soon as bicycles came along the idea was abandoned. Shame, 'cos bouncing along on a Magical Mule is great fun — and those ice cream horns of theirs are yummy.

More recently, Ponies were used to pull delivery carts, but you needed a whole bunch of 'em to move anything more than a few Moshimetres. Besides, Princess Ponies thought the whole kit and caboodle was beneath them. Worse still, Silly Snufflers are slower than turtles in peanut butter!

But what about SkyPonies? Well, they were only discovered recently (by yours truly), so nobody knows what they were up to back in the old days. Floating on Cloud Nine, I reckon.

These days Ponies get to do whatever they like in complete freedom — unless I decide to round up a few for my secret ranch. So, quit horsin' around - giddy up and plant a few seeds.

Angel

the SkyPony

 # 024

Personality: dainty, celestial, secretive

Angel

Habitat

Cloud Nine, high above the Blocky Mountains. I've also spied a few flapping through the Airy Fairy Plains.

Until recently, SkyPonies were mentioned only in Moshi legend. But that was before a whole herd appeared, as if by magic, on a pink cloud, high above Mount Sillimanjaro. These heavenly creatures rarely visit ground level, but when they do, they tell tales of a strange world in the sky where everything is soft and fluffy. I wish I could confirm this. Believe me, I've tried. I once leapt on a SkyPony as it was taking off. It didn't take kindly to having a passenger and bucked me off at 39,000ft! Luckily I had my golf brolly to slow down my fall.

Likes: ☺
Playing the harp and maple syrup.

Dislikes: ☹
Saddlebags and drawing pins.

Other Ponies:

Gigi the Magical Mule	✓
Mr Snoodle the Silly Snuffler	✓
Priscilla the Princess Pony	✓

Code to catch Angel:

HOT SILLY PEPPERS **ANY** + MAGIC BEANS **ANY** + HOT SILLY PEPPERS **ANY**

Gigi

#079

the Magical Mule

Personality: bewitching, charming, graceful

ULTRA RARE

Gigi

I love fairgrounds!

Likes: ☺
Wild fluttercups
and making magical
daisy chains.

Dislikes: ☹
The smell of diesel
and boiled onions.

Magical Mules are powerful Moshlings descended from enchanted carousel horses. I think that's why they trot along humming fairground tunes, occasionally gliding up and down as if still attached to a merry-go-round. Totally bewitching, these elegant gee-gees love ballroom dancing and can even create rainbows. Shame there's no pot of gold at the end!

When I first tried taming a Magical Mule I could have sworn it was a Lunicorn, but then I grabbed its unihorn and realized it was an ice cream cone held on with liquorice shoelaces. Delicious, and it grows back every time you munch it!

Magical Mules eat cotton candy and wild fluttercups and you can only find those in Crystal Grotto near Copperfield Canyon.

Habitat

Code to catch Gigi:

HOT SILLY PEPPERS **BLUE** + MOON ORCHID **RED** + HOT SILLY PEPPERS **YELLOW**

39

Mr Snoodle
the Silly Snuffler

Personality: slumbersome, dawdly, musical

Silly Snufflers are the sleepiest, snuffliest Moshlings around – and their sleepiness is contagious. Whenever a monster walks past, it can't help but yawn, stretch and fall asleep on the spot . . . zzzzz. And that's how Silly Snufflers avoid being caught. By the time the monster wakes up, the Snuffler has slowly shuffled away. I've tried every trick in the book to catch one of these snoozy critters. I even snuck up on one after drinking a gallon of black coffee, but I still nodded off, even though my eyelids were propped open with matchsticks. Foiled again!

Likes: ☺
Life in the slow lane and lullabies.

Dislikes: ☹
Giant Goobledegoofs and modern jazz.

Code to catch Mr Snoodle:

HOT SILLY PEPPERS — **ANY**

+

DRAGON FRUIT — **YELLOW**

+

HOT SILLY PEPPERS — **PURPLE**

ZZZZZZZ

RARE

Sneaking off while
I'm snoozing again . . .

Mr Snoodle

When they're not shuffling
around, Silly Snufflers graze on
the pumpernickel breadcrumbs of
Franzipan farm, playing ice cream
van melodies with their snouts.

Habitat

ZZZZzz

41

Priscilla
the Princess Pony

048

Personality: haughty, fickle, magical

Priscilla

Habitat

Despite their boastful behaviour, I've discovered that Princess Ponies come from a humble area known as Old Knackersville, near Gluey Gulch.

Thought to be descended from royalty, Princess Ponies are always fiddling with their sparkly tiaras, waving their hooves at passers-by and performing pirouettes. If their regal routines fail to impress, prepare to be astounded, because they can make their manes and tails change colour by jingling their jewellery.

One trick ponies? No way! Years ago, I was lucky enough to attend a Princess Pony party. It was a real honour, as I danced with the belle of the ball and was taught how to curtsy like a pony – not easy when you've only got two legs!

Somewhere over the rainbow . . .

Likes: ☺
Sparkly candy apples and winners' rosettes.

Dislikes: ☹
Nosebags (terribly common) and flat shoes.

Code to catch Priscilla:

MOON ORCHID — **ANY** + MOON ORCHID — **ANY** + SNAP APPLE — **YELLOW**

Leo
the Abominable Snowling

 # 098

Personality: perky, misunderstood, lonely

Leo

Likes: ☺
Chomping snowflakes
and snowboarding.

Dislikes: ☹
Yellow snow and grit.

On Mount Sillimanjaro, often near Elder Furi's hut, Abominable Snowlings have also been spotted on the snowy peaks of Music Island.

Habitat

I've no idea why these snow-munching Moshlings are abominable. I've always found them to be extremely friendly. But I enjoy snowy games as much as they do. You see, Abominable Snowlings adore playing in the white stuff. When they're not making ice sculptures or huge snowmen they're chucking snowballs, playing snow angels and decorating their igloos with chocolate sprinkles.

That's because they live on a diet of snow, ice and slush, so everything they make gets eaten before it melts. Next time you see Elder Furi, ask him for some tips, as he has several Snowling neighbours at his mountain retreat.

Bobbi SingSong
the Jollywood Singaling

Personality: jolly, doolally, hyper-energetic

Bobbi
SingSong

JOLLYWOOD

Habitat

Jollywood, of course. But Bobbi should be coming to a town near you very soon!

If you've never been to Jollywood (it is jolly good) chances are you've no idea how famous Bobbi SingSong really is. A legend in his distant homeland this Moshling gooperstar's smash hit 'Welcome to Jollywood' has even been adopted as Jollywood's national anthem. If only he could remember his mantra! Despite his fame Bobbi drives everywhere in his own luxury rickshaw – and I should know because he recently took me for a spin. It was great fun until he started to show me that 'judder sideways' move of his. We nearly ended up in a pothole. Goodness gracious me!

ULTRA RARE

Likes: ☺
Meditating and playing his sitar.

Dislikes: ☹
Wobble-ade and dilly-dallying.

Rofl
the Jabbering Jibberling

Personality: manic, skittish, nonsensical

Rofl

Gloop Soup

I found my first Jabbering Jibberling scurrying around Mouthy Hollow but I believe some live on Music Island.

Habitat

Wind 'em up and watch 'em go! That's the deal with Jabbering Jibberlings. But there's more to these mouthy Moshlings than big smiles and chattering teeth because they are also completely hyperactive. And as soon as they get wound up they can't stop spouting complete gibberish at breakneck speed. I find dousing them in chilled Gloop Soup helps stem the non-stop nonsense. If that fails I use toffee – not to silence the Jibberlings but to stuff in my ears. Mmm, the sound of chatter-free silence!

Likes: ☺
Corn on the cob and tongue-twisters.

Dislikes: ☹
Dental floss and slow-dancing.

Foodies

Feeling peckish? Then you'd best grab yourself a snack, because reading about Foodies is sure to get your tummy rumbling. These edible Moshlings are just about the strangest critters I ever did see. And let me tell you, they really are delicious.

Nobody knows exactly how Foodies came into existence, let alone who decorates them with sprinkles and icing sugar. Whoever it is, I'd sure like to lick their spoon!

Scoff all you like, but I've managed to grab a bite, lick, chomp and nibble of every Foodie out there. And that's no mean feat, because these scrummy things are either Rare or Ultra Rare. If you want to inhale their sugary aroma, you'll need to get your seed combos just right.

Mmm . . . sweet!

If you're lickin' ya lips in anticipation, don't bother. It takes years of experience to get close enough to take a bite out of a foodie. And some of 'em ain't exactly friendly! I've had quite a few run-ins with Psycho Gingerboys (the meanest Moshlings of all) and even Ringy Thingies are not so sweet when you're chasing them across the boiling oil swamps of Greasy Geezer - unless you fancy a face-full of sticky sprinkles. You do?

Then read on . . .

Coolio
the Magical Sparklepop

Personality: deliquescent, cool, upbeat

What do Sparklepops
sing on birthdays?
Freeze a jolly good fello

I know it sounds a trifle absurd, but these tubby
Moshlings are enchanted. Whenever they need to
chill, glittery sparks zing around their slurpy swirls
accompanied by jingly-jangly nursery rhymes. This
happens quite a lot because Magical Sparklepops go
all gloopy if it gets too hot. That's why I always try
to observe them when the sun is coming out. If the
weather won't play ball, I hide behind a snowdrift
and give 'em a quick blast with my hairdryer. It's
sparkletastic! But what's with the funny waddle?
Well, you try walking wearing a wafery tub.

Habitat

Magical Sparklepops prefer chilly
areas - for obvious reasons.
That's why you'll find them
around Knickerbocker Nook in
the Frozen Dessert Desert.

Coolio,
6 months

Likes: ☺
Whackcurrant sauce
and crushed nuts.

Dislikes: ☹
Too much sun and
big tongues.

Twinkle, twinkle little Sparklepop!

RARE

Coolio

Code to catch Coolio:

STAR BLOSSOM

ANY

+

LOVE BERRIES

BLACK

+

SNAP APPLE

PINK

Cutie Pie
the Wheelie YumYum

 # 091

Personality: zoomtastic, chummy, quick-witted

Cutie Pie

Sprinkle-tastic!

ULTRA RARE

Code to catch Cutie Pie:

DRAGON FRUIT

BLUE

+

STAR BLOSSOM

PINK

+

CRAZY DAISY

PURPLE

54

Check out the wheels! These scrumptilicious Moshlings move like lightning. But so would you, if you had turbo-charged sprinkles and a woowoo-ing cherry on your head. Wheelie YumYums are often forced to flee from hungry predators, leaving spongy crumbs in their wake. Follow the trail and you might find one filling up with a few gallons of super-sweet cocoa. I find the only way to keep up with these zippy foodies is to get on my rocket-powered roller skates and give chase. I've never caught one, but those crumbs are delicious!

A cakey aroma often wafts across Ramekin Plain, so I think CutiePie Canyon (where Wheelie YumYums are rumoured to live) could be located nearby.

Habitat

Sprinkles

Likes: ☺
Steaming hot drinks and fancy napkins.

Dislikes: ☹
Silly aprons and chocolate chip traffic cops.

Hansel
the Psycho Gingerboy

 # 059

Personality: disobedient, loutish, rascally

Hansel

Sweet tunes!

RARE

Code to catch Hansel:

DRAGON FRUIT	MAGIC BEANS	MOON ORCHID
ANY	BLACK	BLACK

According to my great uncle's notes, these half-baked hooligans were originally cooked at 180 degrees, deep inside Cookie Crumb Canyon. I'm not convinced, because they seem to pop up everywhere.

Yikes!

Don't be fooled by the fancy frosting and plump raisins; Psycho Gingerboys are naughty little troublemakers. When they're not stealing sweeties and holding up bakeries, they like hanging around on street corners, tripping up passers-by with their delicious-but-deadly candy canes. Crumbs!

Thankfully, Psycho Gingerboys are easy to catch as they can't help dropping yummy crumbs wherever they go. I hear a bunch of 'em are out to get me, because I accidentally squashed one of their pals. Looks like I'll have to fill my water pistol with milk to soften up the biscuity bullies.

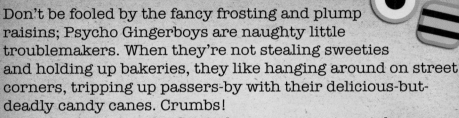

Likes: 😊
Twirling liquorice lassos and bathing in custard

Dislikes: 😟
Cheesy puffs and pecking pigeons.

Oddie
the Sweet Ringy Thingy

#088

Personality: sweet, boisterous, cautious

ULTRA RARE

Oddie's got that glazed look in his eyes again . . . . . .

Oddie

Habitat

I believe Sweet Ringy Thingies are formed and fried in the boiling oil swamps near Greasy Geezer. Exactly who decorates them remains a mystery.

With their doughy bodies and gloopy icing, Sweet Ringy Thingies look exceedingly delicious – and they are! That's why these squishy hoops are always on the move. Everyone wants a piece, especially Moshling collectors who haven't eaten for days. It's a good thing Ringy Thingies can blast attackers with volleys of hundreds and thousands, otherwise they'd be extinct. I've still got a few pink bits stuck in my eyebrows following a recent attack.

If you're wondering how a bunch of sticky doughnutters ever became living, breathing Moshlings, don't. I'm still trying to get to the bottom of it myself.

Likes: 😊
Words beginning with 'O' and hot oil.

Dislikes: 😞
Purple sprouting broccoli and coffee (especially being dunked in it).

Code to catch Oddie:

STAR BLOSSOM
PURPLE
+
STAR BLOSSOM
BLACK
+
STAR BLOSSOM
YELLOW

Plinky
the Squeezy TinkleHuff

 # 106

Personality: gleeful, tuneful, breathless

Plinky

Habitat

TinkleHuffs often busk in Polka Park but they originally come from Hurdy Gurdytown.

'Accordion' to experts (okay, me), these squeezy-wheezy musical Moshlings like nothing more than having their keys tickled as they boing up and down, puffing out merry tunes and waltzing around town. But don't push their buttons – it makes 'em hiccup out of tune. I should know because I used to be a pretty good TinkleHuff player in my youth, but all this newfangled Moshi music has twisted my gooberries and I seem to have lost my touch – maybe I'm too old? One thing certainly hasn't changed – TinkleHuffs are as hard to track down as ever!

Likes: ☺
Waltzing along, squeezing a song.

Dislikes: ☹
Long fingernails and bagpipes.

ULTRA RARE

Blingo
the Flashy Fox

Personality: brash, fast-talking, fashion-conscious

ULTRA RARE

Blingo

Habitat

Likes: ☺
Sharp beard trimmers and chocolate coins.

Dislikes: ☹
Heavy metal and anything made of silver.

Most flashy foxes live up in the Hipsta Hills overlooking Ker-Ching Canyon, but you'll sometimes find a few cruising along Jive Drive.

Slick, cool and super funky, Flashy Foxes never take off their shades. But that's not because it's sunny up in Hipsta Hills, it's because the gleaming bling they collect is totally dazzling! When these hip little Moshlings aren't listening to the latest tunes on their superfly boomboxes, they enjoy hanging out in Horrods and making up silly rhymes in their strange, lightning-fast language. 'Udigwotsgoindown?' I certainly don't, so if I ever need to speak to a Flashy Fox I make sure I always invite my translator, Dr. Unwin Babble.

SECRET

Other Secrets:

Roxy the Precious Prism	✓

Cherry Bomb

the Baby Boomer

Personality: sparky, bombastic, loud

Cherry Bomb

ALARM

RARE

Stick your fingers in your ears, the Baby Boomers are here! But don't panic, these clockwork Moshlings rarely go boom. The reason they're so noisy is because their fuses fizz and crackle whenever they're excited. I found this out the hard way when I was exploring the Candy Cane Caves and tried to entice a Baby Boomer out from its hidey-hole with a bowl of kaboomalot custard. Big mistake because it got so excited its fizzly fuse sparked an explosion. My eyebrows have never been the same.

Fzzzttt!

Baby Boomers can pop up anywhere (yikes!) but often fizzle around Kaboom Canyon.

Habitat

Likes: ☺
Bangers and crash with dynamite sauce.

Dislikes: ☹
Buckets of water and candle snuffers.

Ninjas

Legend has it that somewhere over the rainbow, in the Land of the Surprising Sun, Ninja Moshlings once lived together, training, meditating and chopping planks of wood in half with their heads. These days, Ninjas aren't half as silly — they are ten times worse.

Hi-yaaa!

Most of them wear bandanas, hoods or helmets because they think it's good for their stealth. But the truth is, you can spot a Ninja a mile off — even Caped Assassins can't help popping up when they are supposed to be hiding. And Cheeky Chimps can't resist playing pranks and shouting 'boo!'

s for Warrior Wombats, well, they might be Ultra Rare but these noble Moshlings spend most days snoozing. Slapstick Tortoises? They are too busy having mishaps to do much at all.

Apart from a love of sushi and badly dubbed kung-fu movies, the one thing that links Ninjas together, even today, is their ability to speak ancient Moshlingese — a strange language that even I struggle to get my tongue around.

Chop Chop

the Cheeky Chimp

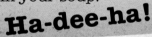

Monkeying around

Personality: ninjarish, naughty, impish

As well as being part-time ninjas, Cheeky Chimps are full-time jokers. They leave a telltale trail of whoopee cushions, banana skins and stink bombs wherever they roam. In fact, these playful primates don't know when to stop. And that can be pretty funny, unless the joke's on me.

Over the years I've been pelted with gooberries, squirted by plastic flowers and even had ink smeared around my spinoculars. Watch out, or you could end up with a face-full of custard pie and a rubber chicken in your soup.

Ha-dee-ha!

Habitat

Most Cheeky Chimps swing through the vines of Sniggerton Wood, but some prefer hiding in closets before jumping out and shouting 'Boo!'

What did the banana say to the monkey?
Nothing. Bananas don't talk.

Likes: ☺
Tying shoelaces together and flicking ears.

Dislikes: ☹
Political talk shows and runny porridge.

Category: Ninjas

Chop Chop

Code to catch Chop Chop:

 **+**  **+**

DRAGON FRUIT — ANY

DRAGON FRUIT — ANY

DRAGON FRUIT — ANY

General Fuzuki
the Warrior Wombat

Personality: serious, mysterious, reliable

ULTRA RARE

General Fuzuki

Knock! Knock!
Who's there?
Warrior
Warrior who?
Warrior you been all my life!

Catchin' some ZZZZZZs

Code to catch General Fuzuki:

HOT SILLY PEPPERS

RED

+

LOVE BERRIES

YELLOW

+

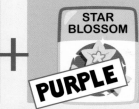

STAR BLOSSOM

PURPLE

I heard a rumour that Warrior Wombats were once used to guard Rox and other precious things. But that's not because these furry little Moshlings are fearless. It's because legend has it they don't need any sleep. Or do they? My research shows that their 'open eyes' are actually titchy cake tins welded to their hats. This allows them to take forty winks on the sly. Napping on the job? Now that's naughty. Still, at least it helps me study the rare little sleepyheads. I just sneak up with my snore-o-meter and get busy.

Warrior Wombats live in the sub-zero wastelands of ChillyBot State Park, a mysterious place where darkness never falls. Pack your shades!

Habitat

Likes: ☺
Shiny objects and comfy cushions.

Dislikes: ☹
Alarm clocks and bits of food in beards.

Sooki-Yaki
the Caped Assassin # 047

Personality: stealthy, wide-eyed 'n' bushy-tailed, evanescent

Sooki-
Yaki

If cars run on petrol and cookers run on gas, what do caped assassins run on? Their paws!

Code to catch Sooki - Yaki:

HOT SILLY PEPPERS
ANY

+

MAGIC BEANS
ANY

+

MAGIC BEANS
RED

Most Caped Assassin sightings have been reported near East Grumble. If you're lucky, you might see one suddenly appear halfway up a drainpipe. I have and it scared me silly!

Habitat

Now you see them, now you still see them! And that's because Caped Assassins are not as good at sneaking around as they think they are. Don't laugh, because these agile little Moshlings possess the ability to vanish and reappear in an instant. They don't even register on my Moshling detector.

The problem is, they can't control their power and always pop up when they shouldn't. I should know, because the first Caped Assassin I ever saw appeared right in front of me just as it was about to . . . er, well I never found out. It disappeared again.

Likes: ☺
Gadgets and knitting.

Dislikes: ☹
Itchy collars and slippery roof tiles.

Shelby
the Slapstick Tortoise

 # 039

Personality: bonkers, clumsy, gormless

Shelby

What was the tortoise doing on the motorway About fifty millimetres an hour!

Shelby, age 5 months

74

Slapstick Tortoises are highly-trained Moshlings. It's just a shame whoever trained them was dumb as a stump. The only thing they're good at is messing up their moves and tumbling on to their wobbly shells. They can't even tie their own bandanas. And that's bad because they're supposed to be ninjas. If only they stopped watching silly kung-fu movies, they wouldn't be so useless.

I encountered my first Slapstick Tortoise whilst collecting shrillberries. In fact, I nearly trod on it because it was flailing around belly-side up.

Hi-yaaa!

Likes: ☺
Brushing their teeth with toffee and buffing up their shells.

Dislikes: ☹
Laying belly-side up and jogging.

These gormless Moshlings hibernate under the boardwalk at Groan Bay but often gather to compare (and then mess up) new fighting moves at the Wailing Wharf.

Habitat

Code to catch Shelby:

DRAGON FRUIT	MAGIC BEANS	DRAGON FRUIT
ANY	ANY	BLACK

Wallop
the Jolly Tubthumper

Personality: energetic, rackety, raucous

Wallop

When they're not on tour, Jolly Tubthumpers are believed to live in Thwackboom Valley.

Habitat

Crash, bang, Wallop? Absolutely, because Jolly Tubthumpers are the stick-wielding Tunies who are always on the beat. Okay, so bashing yourself in the face with a pair of drumsticks isn't crazy – it's totally bonkers. But where else are these tip-tapping Moshlings supposed to practise their paradiddles? Besides, Jolly Tubthumpers love drumming, and their thwacktastic bodies are brilliantly boingy. They even made a guest appearance on the Super Moshi March. I have several on my secret ranch and often get them to play a few drum fills to cheer up their fellow Moshlings. They love it. I think. Drum roll please!

Likes: ☺
Twirling sticks and marching for miles.

Dislikes: ☹
Being shhh'd and blisters.

Shelly
the Nattering Nutling

Personality: excitable, gossipy, swooning

Shelly

Bobbi Singsong

Missy Kix

Zack Binspin

78

Nattering Nutlings can usually be found flicking through the latest Ruby Scribblez book in Goober Gulch.

Habitat

Completely nuts? Not exactly but Nattering Nutlings are definitely crazy . . . about Moshi celebrities! And that's bad news for me because thanks to my bestselling guidebooks I'm a household name these days. Whenever I get close to one of these gossipy Moshlings the first thing it does is flutter its eyelashes and ask for an autograph before running off screaming. Goodness knows how a Nutling would react if it bumped into a proper star like Zack Binspin. When they're not singing Music Rox songs in front of the mirror, Nattering Nutlings love chattering to each other about the hottest new gooperstars.

Likes: ☺
Gossip columns and jam.

Dislikes: ☹
Salt and Cheeky Chimps.

Jessie
the Ginger McMoshling

Personality: testy, buffoonish, lively

Jessie

Habitat

Ginger McMoshlings can be found bobbing about on Loch Mess but some play golf near McHaggis Castle on Music Island.

80

Thought to be distant descendants of the legendary Sock Less Monster, Ginger McMoshlings look a bit like mini Jabbersauruses – ancient creatures that roamed the world of Moshi before the Great Custard Flood. All I know for sure is that these tartan-clad critters love a wee jig whenever they hear the drone of the sagpipes. Believe me, there is nothing funnier than the sight of a very merry McMoshling performing a Highland fling, especially if it decides to pull off its false beard (which is glued to its hat) and wear it as a kind of kilt.

Och-aye!

Likes: 🙂 Shortbread biscuits and misty mornings.

Dislikes: 🙁 Trousers and shandy.

What do you get if you feed the Loch Ness Monster mutant sprouts?
The Loch Ness Pongster

ULTRA RARE

Fluffies

If you're looking for cuddles, you've come to the right place! Fluffies are soft, squishy and impossibly cute. I still wouldn't recommend snuggling one until you are an expert collector — some of 'em bite and some have thundery tempers.

Take IGGY. This Ultra Rare Pixel-Munching Snaffler just loves scoffing pointy arrows (cursors, I think you keyboard-tappers call 'em). Anyhow, little IGGY (short for "I'm Gonna Get Ya") is quite a handful and often pops up out of nowhere, vanishing before you can say 'control', 'alt' or even 'delete'.

Far more relaxed are Honey and Flumpy. These snugglesome Fluffies are friendly as can be. Which is more than can be said for Dipsy. Don't get me wrong, this weeny wisp of mysterious fluff is mostly angelic. Trouble is, she tends to pou with rain the second she is upset.

Although Fluffies can be found all over the land of Moshi, I don't think they are of this world. I reckon they originated from deep within the Squishy Dream Dimension, an ultra-squashy place that only appears if you close your eyes and cuddle your pillow. Awww, cute!

Dipsy
the Dinky Dreamcloud

Personality: jolly, capricious, fanciful

Dipsy

Aah, ickle flurry cloud!

Habitat

Dinky Dreamclouds are native to Meringue Meadow, an area surrounded by towering vanilla pod trees and wild candiflop.

Likes: ☺
Doing the splits and marmalade with bits.

Dislikes: ☹
Modern dance and clumpy shoes.

84

Dinky Dreamclouds dream of becoming Ginormous Dreamclouds, but they are far too teeny for such an important job. That's why they flutter and flap about all day, making cute noises and admiring their eyelashes.

Don't get them angry, or they might rain on you – something I discovered when I tried to poke one with my telescopic Moshling prod. The fluffy little creature hovered over my head for the rest of the expedition, bucketing down on me every time I tried to shoo it away. Worst of all, I'd forgotten my umbrella.

Aah-choo!

Other Fluffies:

Flumpy the Pluff	
Honey the Funny Bunny	✓
IGGY (or "I'm Gonna Get Ya")	✓
	✓

The Pixel-Munching Snaffler

Code to catch Dipsy:

MOON ORCHID **ANY** + LOVE BERRIES **ANY** + MOON ORCHID **YELLOW**

Flumpy
the Pluff
054

Personality: cheerful, carefree, big-hearted

Habitat

Pluffs originally come from the Cotton Clump plantations, but you'll often see them strolling around town, smiling at the world.

Many monsters think Pluffs are the most chilled-out Moshlings of all. And it's hard to disagree when you see them strolling through the Cotton Clump plantations, arms dangling, grinning as if they haven't a care in the world. If you want to chillax, you can't beat hanging out with a gang of Pluffs.

I've enjoyed many a sunny afternoon stretched out on my deckchair 'researching' these friendly Fluffies. They don't even mind when I take photos and ask them to sign my postcards. Wish you were here? It's a tough job, but someone's gotta do it.

Likes: ☺
Rubber gloves and furniture polish.

Dislikes: ☹
Clutter and the smell of damp.

RARE **Flumpy**

What's white and fluffy?
Flumpy.
What's blue and fluffy?
Flumpy holding its breath!

Code to catch Flumpy:

STAR BLOSSOM
ANY

+

MAGIC BEANS
RED

+

MOON ORCHID
BLACK

Honey
the Funny Bunny

#057

Personality: outgoing, natty, chatty

Honey

RARE

Code to catch Honey:

MAGIC BEANS

ANY

+

LOVE BERRIES

YELLOW

+

SNAP APPLE

BLUE

You might expect these rabbity Moshlings to live in basic burrows, but most of them own incredibly modern hutches in Pawberry Fields.

Habitat

What's Honey's favourite game?
Hopscotch!

Dedicated followers of fashion, Funny Bunnies are the best-dressed Moshlings in town. Yes, I know that's hard to believe looking at my stylish outfit, but it's true. I'm pretty sure they think I'm hip. Well, they always chuckle and point when they see me.

If they're not busy texting jokes to their friends, these incredibly cute furballs can be found yacking about carrot cake, clothes and fur straighteners. Talking of straightening, all Funny Bunnies have one floppy ear. I'm convinced this is caused by listening to silly ringtones all day.

Likes: ☺
Sniggering at silly jokes and ironing flowers (especially naffodils).

Dislikes: ☹
Orange sauce and lukewarm nincomsoup.

IGGY
100
the Pixel-Munching Snaffler

Personality: unpredictable, hyper, bouncy

Aargh! Curse those pesky cursors!
   These pixel-scoffing Moshlings look innocent enough, but the second they spot a pointy arrow, it's history. I've spoken to a few keyboard-tapping geeks and they believe Snafflers find computer cursors really annoying – like flies flittering around their heads. But seeing as they can't swat them (they've got no arms, let alone rolled-up newspapers) they gobble them up. It's not just arrows though: my precious hat has been munched from my head on several occasions. It must taste funny, because the Snafflers always spit it straight out.

Yuck!

Habitat

You might occasionally spot a Pixel-Munching Snaffler trapped in a hedge, but they usually whoosh in from mysterious portals in cyberspace, called Aargates.

Likes: ☺
Power surges and tickly pickles.

Dislikes: ☹
Delete keys and nifty mouse-operators.

t many people know
his, but IGGY stands
or 'I'm Gonna Get Ya!'

ULTRA RARE

IGGY

Spit out my cursor!

Code to catch IGGY:

MOON ORCHID — **BLACK** + CRAZY DAISY — **PURPLE** + CRAZY DAISY — **PURPLE**

Cute and cuddly? Maybe, but there's no time for snuggles when you are searching for Fluffies. I've had some of my greatest adventures trapping these little softies . . .

This afternoon I managed to snaffle the Ultra Rare IGGY - and I'm not even a computer geek! I stuck an arrow-shaped bit of card to a glueberry bush and waited for the greedy gobbler to pounce. The second it took a bite outta my pretend cursor, it was stuck. Lemme tell ya, that pesky varmint was madder than a mule chewing bumblebees. Gotcha!

It must be my lucky week Fluffie-wise, because yesterday I collected several Funny Bunnies using a newfangled contraption called a 'mobile phone'. I just sent a text telling them where to meet and herded them straight into the party prairie on my Moshling ranch. They were too busy nattering, texting and nibbling my home-baked carrot cake to notice.

As for Dinky Dreamclouds, to avoid getting drenched I find it's always best to entice them down to ground level with marmalade and wild candiflop. I also pack an umbrella, just to be on the safe side.

But how about Pluffs? Well, there's no need to go chasing these easy-going Moshlings. They are happy to do whatever I tell 'em. Why, I'm resting my tired tootsies on a snoozing Pluff as I write this very page.

Yes, siree, Pluffs and Buster go together like grits and gravy. "Hey Flumpy, don't forget to massage this here little piggy that went to market."

Rooby

the Plucky PunchaRoo

 # 062

Personality: bouncy, plucky, protective

Rooby

Habitat

From the fabled land Downunder, where didgeridoos blow and skies thunder.

94

Say g'day and duck out the way because Plucky PunchaRoos are the paw-swinging Moshlings that will do almost anything to protect the titchy purple critters that live in their pouches. And that's strange because the purple critters are actually soft toys stuffed with jellybeans. Capable of flummoxing almost any Monster with their lightning fast fists and fancy footwork, PunchaRoos love a scrap. I once challenged one to a bout of fisticuffs but it refused – something about not wanting to wallop a creaky old-timer.

What a cheek!

Nothing parts Rooby from his jellybeans!

Likes: ☺
Barbecues and boomerangs.

Dislikes: ☹
Smelling salts and daytime soap operas.

RARE

Gracie

the Swishy Missy

Personality: graceful, talented, determined

Gracie

You can often spot the glint of a Swishy Missy's magic tiara on the Frostipop Glacier but these graceful Moshlings can be found anywhere, skates and all!

Habitat

Get your skates on! If you wanna catch a Swishy Missy you'll need to be an expert on the ice. These figure-skating Moshlings are unstoppable. When they are not twirling, jumping and performing toe-jumps on the Frostipop Glacier, Swishies are, erm, pretty clumsy. That's because they refuse to take their magic skates off, even at bedtime. I once danced with a Swishy Missy on a frozen puddle but made rather a fool of myself when my trousers split as I was attempting a triple axel. Luckily I'd ironed my underpants.

How embarrassing!

Swishing elegantly across the ice - nice!

Likes: ☺
Sequins and heavy eye make-up.

Dislikes: ☹
Low scoring judges and slush.

Fizzy

the Lipsmacking Bubbly

Personality: effervescent, zany, unpredictable

Thirsty? You'd better be careful if a Lipsmacking Bubbly offers you a drink because these madcap Moshlings are fizzy beyond belief. In fact, the bendy straw poking out of every Bubbly's lid is not just for sipping. It allows the gas from all that fizzy-wizzy pop to escape so that they don't blow their tops. I often take a few of these crazy critters on expeditions as their bubbly behaviour is highly refreshing, especially if I feed them peppermints because this causes a sparkling eruption of delicious pop. Sweet fizzy rain on a hot day? What could be better!

Habitat

Lipsmacking Bubblies are rumoured to hang out in CutiePie Canyon but they can also be found in Uppity Cup Creek.

RARE

Fizzy

Likes: ☺
Mints and the taste of cardboard.

Dislikes: ☹
Wasps and ringpulls.

Fishies

Even if you've never studied fishtory, you don't need to be a brain sturgeon to know what links Fishies together. Give up? It's big, blue and really wobbly. No, not the cashier at Yukea, I'm talking about the ocean. So slip on your flippers, suck on your snorkel and listen up!

These sub-aquatic Moshlings can't get enough of the beautiful briny sea — or anything else that's remotely wet. But that doesn't stop 'em ploppin' above the surface whenever it tickles their fins.

I've seen Acrobatic SeaStars somersaulting along Main Street and Valley Mermaids eating seaweed sandwiches by Firebreath Fountain. (Then again, I had been drinking Wobble-ade in the Aargh Bar that night.)

Speaking of mermaids, the enormous Sea Mall deep beneath Potion Ocean is their fave new hangout. But you're just as likely to see a Songful Seahorse bobbing along the aisles whilst a Batty Bubblefish shops for ink refills.

As you can tell, Fishies get along famously. Well, the ones on the following pages do — because although I've identified just four 'offishal' species, I'm pretty sure there are plenty more fish in the sea. So, watch this space — failing that, go jump in a lake.

Glug!

Blurp
the Batty Bubblefish

Personality: scatty, crotchety, bewildered

Blurp

Watch out, wormy!

Icky gloop – yuck!

Code to catch Blurp:

MOON ORCHID **ANY** + LOVE BERRIES **ANY** + LOVE BERRIES **PINK**

Category: Fishies

All puffed-up with nowhere to blow, Batty Bubblefish spend most days swimming around in circles holding their breath. In fact, these marine Moshlings have got such terrible memories they can't remember what it is they're supposed to have forgotten. A bit like me!

Never upset one, as they can splurt out gallons of multi-coloured gloop – something I learnt the hard way when I tried to examine one with my giant underwater fish spatula. It took me months to get that stuff outta my whiskers. Still, at least I won't forget the incident – I've got a nasty stain on my swimsuit to remind me!

Stand back, he's ready to blow!

Habitat

Likes: ☺
Old flip-flops and . . . erm, can't remember.

Dislikes: ☹
Fish fingers and swallowing water.

Batty Bubblefish live in the foamy waters beneath Fruit Falls. Hang around and you might see one leap out of the water, blow a raspberry and plop back under.

Cali
the Valley Mermaid

Personality: ditzy, sassy, caffeinated

RARE

Cali

STARFISHBUCKS COFFEE

Habitat

You can find Valley Mermaids flouncing around the new Sea Mall deep beneath Potion Ocean.

To use Valley Mermaid lingo, 'Like, wow . . . there's something totally fishy going on here.' Confused? Me too. I need to consult my mermaid translation book every time I hear one of these ditzy fishies speak. Maybe I'm getting old. What-ever!

When they're not freaking out over the latest koi band or knocking back cappuccinos at the local Starfishbucks, these hip little cuties love hooking up fellow Moshlings.

In fact, their hearts flash whenever they sense romance. Lucky for me they are usually too busy yacking to notice this old timer scribbling notes.

Duh!

Likes: ☺
Seaweed sandwiches and chilling out in crates of ice.

Dislikes: ☹
The Boogie Woogie Bluegill Boys and rusty anchors.

What did the sea say to the mermaid? Nothing, it just waved!

Code to catch Cali:

MAGIC BEANS		LOVE BERRIES		LOVE BERRIES
ANY	+	**YELLOW**	+	**BLUE**

Fumble
the Acrobatic SeaStar

Personality: gnarly, fearless, full of beans

Gimme five! Or four? Or how about three? Because when they're not cartwheeling along the seabed performing death-defying stunts, Acrobatic SeaStars spend most days gluing their pointy bits back on. They're a bit accident-prone, you see. Thing is, they can't resist showing-off, even if it means tumbling face-first into a pile of poisonous seagrass. Now that's gotta hurt!

A while back, I got mixed up in a crazy pile-up when I was snorkelling in Potion Ocean; a troupe of SeaStars bungeed off a coral formation straight onto my head. Luckily I still had my trusty hat on.

These energetic Moshling live amongst the coral reefs of Bleurgh Lagoon but often gather on the beach to body surf.

Habitat

Likes: ☺
Removing bandages and thrash metal.

Dislikes: ☹
Safety nets and outboard motors.

RARE

Fumble

Code to catch Fumble:

STAR BLOSSOM	LOVE BERRIES	MAGIC BEANS
ANY	YELLOW	YELLOW

Stanley #018
the Songful SeaHorse

What's the difference between a fish and a piano? You can't tuna fish!

Personality: flamboyant, tactless, ear-splittingly noisy

Splish, splash! Stanley taking a bath!

Stanley

Putting out fires!

Category: Fishies

Songful SeaHorses are not very good swimmers so they usually bob around the shallow waters of Reggae Reef. Failing that, look in the bath.

Habitat

Although they are very cute, Songful SeaHorses can be incredibly annoying. That's because they can't stop whistling awful show tunes really loudly. Each ear-splitting ditty is usually accompanied by a barrage of bubbles and a silly dance. My research suggests they are trying to attract other SeaHorses, but I've been unable to stand the racket long enough to confirm this. Even earmuffs are useless. That's why I've invented a special squishy snout plug to muffle their trumpety blasts. All I need now is a volunteer to sneak up and plop it in. Any takers?

Likes: ☺
Kazoo concertos and sea oats.

Dislikes: ☹
Bubble bath and serious opera.

Code to catch Stanley:

DRAGON FRUIT — ANY **+** LOVE BERRIES — ANY **+** LOVE BERRIES — ANY

Pip
the Savvy Sapling

Personality: enthusiastic, caring, curious

Pip

Habitat

Why did the leaf go to the doctor?

It was feeling a little green!

The main Savvy Sapling village is hidden in undergrowth in Wobbly Woods but Shrewman tells me they also live in hidey-holes in the trees.

Category: Nutties

Savvy by name, savvy by nature, these titchy woodland Moshlings know everything there is to know (and maybe a bit more) about nature. When they are not studying soil samples, leaping into piles of leaves and collecting berries in their little acorn hats, Savvy Saplings enjoy playing golf with twiggy clubs and mini gooberry balls. I once stumbled across a tournament and got pelted on the backside with a splat attack of berries. Luckily the Savvy Saplings soon realised I was a fellow nature expert and decided to compare notes. Fascinating, especially as theirs were written in enchanted sap.

Likes: ☺
Raindrops and conkers.

Dislikes: ☹
Concrete and Moshling collectors with big feet.

TOP SECRET

Judder
the Unhinged Jackhammer

Personality: crazed, jittery, irritating

Judder

UNDER CONSTRUCTION

Originally from McQuiver Quarry, Unhinged Jackhammers can be found wherever there are roadworks to be done.

Habitat

H-h-hold on a s-s-sec. I'm sh-sh-shuddering because I've just b-b-been chatting to an Unhinged Jackhammer. These manic Moshlings just love boinging up and down, even when there isn't a road to ruin. Used by Roarkers to smash up the streets of Monstro City and beyond, Unhinged Jackhammers should be handled with care, because once they start juddering they ignore everything else around them. I once made the mistake of disturbing a sleeping Jackhammer and ended up hanging onto its ears for dear life as it pogoed along Main Street.

Likes: ☺
Burst water pipes and traffic cones.

Dislikes: ☹
Car horns and traffic jams.

Tingaling

 # 063

the Kitten of Good Fortune

Personality: generous, friendly, wise

Tingaling

Other Luckies:

Penny the Mini Money	✓

Likes: ☺
Reading tea leaves and scoffing fortune cookies.

Dislikes: ☹
Investigative journalists and Moshling Puppies.

Hong Bong Island

Good fortune befalls any monster who stumbles upon a Kitten of Good Fortune, particularly if its magic neck bell is tinkling. I first came across one of these incredibly cute little Moshlings whilst dining in a restaurant on Hong Bong Island, in the middle of Potion Ocean. I'm not sure if its mystical powers had any effect, but I do remember finding a pile of Rox in my rucksack shortly afterwards, so who knows? Remember to wave if you see one because these mystic Moshlings can spread joy and happiness with just one wave of the paw.

RARE

Tyra's Spa

Habitat

Originally from Hong Bong Island, Kittens of Good Fortune love relaxing on windowsills and rooftops.

Spookies

Woo-ooh! You can come out from behind the sofa — Spookies aren't that scary. Okay, these supernatural Moshlings can be a little creepy, but most of them are pretty friendly. Well, kind of.

I must admit I didn't believe in ghosts - let alone little Banshees, Hoodoos and Heebees — till I spotted something drifting past my tent one stormy night during an expedition to Fang-Ten Valley.

Turns out it was one of them there pesky Squidge critters trying to drain ol' Buster dry. Lucky I sleep with my scarf on and my tent zipped - no bloodsucker's getting its teeth into this here juicy neck!

Since then I've learnt everything there is to know about Spookies. These mysterious Moshlings can plop out of plasma clouds, drift through walls, cast spells, turn you inside out and give even the bravest of collectors the willies.

But not me, oh no. Thanks to my nerves of steel I've caught ghosties galore and . . . Aargh! What was that? Oh, it's just my jimmy jams flapping on the clothes line. Where was I? Oh yes, on the following pages I'll tell you what seeds you need to start collecting Spookies. So don't be a scaredy-cat, get huntin'.

Mwah-ha-ha!

Big Bad Bill #089
the Woolly Blue Hoodoo

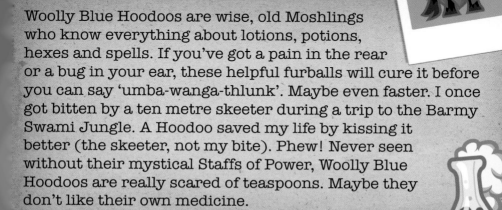

Personality: wise, mystical, generous

Woolly Blue Hoodoos are wise, old Moshlings who know everything about lotions, potions, hexes and spells. If you've got a pain in the rear or a bug in your ear, these helpful furballs will cure it before you can say 'umba-wanga-thlunk'. Maybe even faster. I once got bitten by a ten metre skeeter during a trip to the Barmy Swami Jungle. A Hoodoo saved my life by kissing it better (the skeeter, not my bite). Phew! Never seen without their mystical Staffs of Power, Woolly Blue Hoodoos are really scared of teaspoons. Maybe they don't like their own medicine.

Naturally nomadic, Woolly Blue Hoodoos wander vast areas in search of enlightenment and bald peaches. According to my great uncle's notes, they come from a lost tribe found deep in the Gombala Gombala Jungle.

Habitat

Likes: ☺
Deep massage and deep-fried Oobla Doobla.

Dislikes: ☹
Clowns and itchy eyeballs.

ULTRA RARE

Big Bad Bill

Code to catch Big Bad Bill:

STAR BLOSSOM

BLUE

+

LOVE BERRIES

YELLOW

+

STAR BLOSSOM

BLACK

Ecto
the Fancy Banshee

060

Personality: ephemeral, spooky, silent

RARE

Ecto

Habitat

Scientists can scoff, but I think Fancy Banshees come from a parallel vortex deep within the ClothEar Cloud Formation. It can only be accessed by running around shouting "woo-oo-oo" really loudly.

Psst . . . don't be afraid, Fancy Banshees are quite friendly. Just make sure you don't touch one, because their shimmering capes are made of electrified wobble-plasma, mysterious stuff that turns things inside-out. How do I know? Yep, you guessed it, I got Ectoed! It happened when I was exploring Collywobbles Castle. I never did find my compass. Or my back teeth.

When they're not drifting through walls in the dead of night, these totally silent Moshlings float around collecting Rox dust. No one knows why, but I believe they need to absorb it to keep glowing.

Likes: ☺
Rox dust and darkness.

Dislikes: ☹
Anyone called Ichabod and being upside-down.

What's Ecto's favourite fruit?
Booberries!

Code to catch Ecto:

HOT SILLY PEPPERS

ANY

LOVE BERRIES

RED

LOVE BERRIES

BLACK

Kissy
the Baby Ghost

Personality: cute, frangible, shy

Kissy

Kissy's favourite bedtime story is *Ghouldilocks and the Three Scares*.

122

These charming Moshlings plop out of the plasma clouds high above the abandoned Harem Scarum pickling plant in the Okay-ish Lands.

Habitat

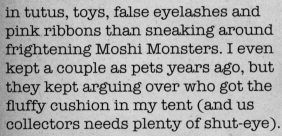

It's hard being scary when you're as cute as a Baby Ghost. These supernatural Moshlings are more interested in tutus, toys, false eyelashes and pink ribbons than sneaking around frightening Moshi Monsters. I even kept a couple as pets years ago, but they kept arguing over who got the fluffy cushion in my tent (and us collectors needs plenty of shut-eye).

If you do see a Baby Ghost, try not to breathe near it, or it might evaporate, leaving just a bow and a pair of soggy pink pumps. I think that's what happened to mine.

Oops!

Likes: ☺
Fluffy poodles and loganberry lip gloss.

Dislikes: ☹
Suction cups and sponges.

Code to catch Kissy:

STAR BLOSSOM	MAGIC BEANS	STAR BLOSSOM
ANY	ANY	PURPLE

Squidge

the Furry Heebee

Personality: diabolical, creepy, bitey-witey

Squidge

Code to catch Squidge:

HOT SILLY PEPPERS
ANY

+

STAR BLOSSOM
ANY

+

DRAGON FRUIT
ANY

It's rare to see a Furry Heebee at all, but if you do it will be hanging upside-down in the Crazy Caves of Fang-Ten Valley.

Habitat

Super-cute? Not really. A Furry Heebee's bite is worse than its bark. That's because these flying Moshlings are greedy bloodsuckers that flutter around after dark hunting for juicy victims. I never go looking for them without my splat-tastic swatter, and I always wear a polo neck jumper. When they can't find any necks to nip, Heebees will settle for a nice mug of instant tomato soup with plenty of garlicky croutons – and that's how I catch 'em. Oh yes, about the bark: it's more of a high-pitched "mwah-ha-ha", but it's still enough to give you goosebumps!

Likes: ☺
Long capes and scary organ music.

Dislikes: ☹
Heebee-repellent spray and figures-of-eight.

HipHop

the Blaring Boombox

Personality: retro, noisy, funky

Say 'wassup' to Blaring Boomboxes, the playful noisemakers who just can't stop rockin' to the bang beat boogie that blares from their speakers day and night. Obsessed with old-school tunes, they love sharing their music with other Moshlings – and that can be mighty annoying because Grandmaster Bash and his Furious Hive (legendary Moshi rapper with a beehive hairdo) is no longer popular in Monstro City. If you're feeling daring you can always reach for the 'stop' button (every Blaring Boombox has one on its head). Just make sure you don't press 'record' as this causes them to lose their memory.

Oops!

Likes: ☺
Skipping rope and bustin' rhymes.

Dislikes: ☹
Flat batteries and MP3s.

HipHop

Habitat

TinnyTone Boulevard, but I've also spotted Blaring Boomboxes hanging out in Hipsta Hills with Flashy Foxes.

Tomba
the Wistful Snowtot  # 066

Personality: frosty, shy, melancholy

Tomba

RARE

Category: Snowies

On Mount Sillimanjaro but they sometimes migrate (to go curling) on the Frostipop Glacier.

Habitat

Feeling chilly? There must be a Wistful Snowtot nearby because these frosty little Moshlings are made of ice, snow and stuff we don't know. As their name suggests, they're usually glum – hardly surprising when abominable critters are always kicking them to bits. Worse still, they can only smell carrots. Heartbrrr-eaking! Not so long ago I met a few Snowtots on the set of a Twistmas video they were appearing in. It was a far cry from my first encounter with these chilly chappies – I slipped on a frozen puddle of Snowtot tears whilst exploring ChillyBot State Park.

Ouch!

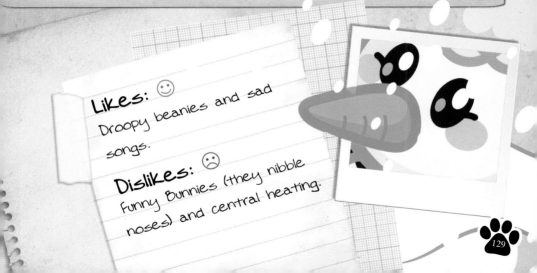

Likes: ☺
Droopy beanies and sad songs.

Dislikes: ☹
Funny Bunnies (they nibble noses) and central heating.

129

CocoLoco
the Naughty Nutter
109

Personality: nutty, rowdy, playful

ULTRA RARE

Fancy a drink? You're in good company because Naughty Nutters can't stop sipping bongo-colada from their nutty heads. It's refreshing stuff but I believe it makes them slightly nuts – the last time I had a slurp I woke up in a hammock with vague memories of conga-ing, limbo-ing and partying the night away. Worse still, all I could hear was funky rattling. I later discovered Naughty Nutters love shaking home-made maracas filled with thumpkin seeds the second the sun rises. And if you think that's annoying, wait till you're forced to do the bossanova over breakfast!

Likes: ☺
Hula dancing and ukuleles.

Dislikes: ☹
Curly straws and pork scratchings.

CocoLoco

On Hoohah Husk trees in the Gombala Gombala Jungle and in the Unknown Zone on Music Island.

Habitat

131

Birdies

Squawk! Apart from beaks, wings and feathers, Birdie Moshlings have got little in common. Stunt Penguins can't even fly! (Well, they can, but piloting old-fashioned biplanes doesn't really count.) In fact, the only time Birdies get together is for the annual Birdie Bash, a crazy rave hosted by Disco Duckies over on the TakiTaki Islands.

But things used to be very different. Oodles of years ago, all four Birdie species lived together in Fluttertown, an ancient tree-village that is now submerged, deep beneath Lake Inferior.

Birdie life was much the same as it is today: Pilfering Toucans would steal sunglasses from Disco Duckies (who in those days were known as Classical Quackers), Stunt Penguins would torment Sabre-toothed Splatterpillars and Owls of Wiseness would occasionally look up from their books to tut.

According to legend, the Birdies went their separate ways after the devastating Moshi custard flood of 99999.5. These days, although they don't really mix, Birdies can be found flapping, waddling, swooping and sliding all over the world of Moshi, from Wobbly Woods to Lush Lagoon. Plant the right seeds and you might see one sooner than you think.

Look, up in the sky. . .

DJ Quack
the Disco Duckie

Personality: funky, big-headed, completely quackers

DJ Quack

Disco Duckies live on the TakiTaki Islands in the middle of Lake Neon Soup.
Well, it's more of a pond really, but don't tell them that.

Habitat

134

You can tell by the way they waddle that these groovy little quackers were born to boogie. Matter of fact, I had to wear purple legwarmers and blow on a funky whistle to bag my first Disco Duckie. And what a jive-quacking critter it was!

When they're not flapping around mirrorballs and dipping their beaks in glittery gloop, these music-mad Moshlings are busy busting out new dance moves and slicking back their feathers with orange sauce. If you ever meet one in a dark alley, be sure to duck – they can't see a thing with those shades on.

Likes: ☺
Quacking in time to the beat and moonwalking.

Dislikes: ☹
Silence and getting peanut butter stuck in their beaks.

Get down to the underground disco!

Code to catch DJ Quack:

DRAGON FRUIT	MOON ORCHID	STAR BLOSSOM
ANY	ANY	ANY

Peppy
the Stunt Penguin

Personality: reckless, rebellious, wheely obsessive

Peppy

RARE

Code to catch Peppy:

MOON ORCHID	MAGIC BEANS	MOON ORCHID
ANY	YELLOW	RED

136

Despite being rubbish at riding bikes (their feet don't reach the pedals), these cool little Moshlings are obsessed by anything with two or more wheels. That's why they slide along on their tummies making vroom-vroom noises and revving the air with their stumpy wings. One dotty daredevil even tried to climb aboard my MoshiMobile, but couldn't find the keys.

As well as their need for speed, Stunt Penguins love scoffing pilchard popsicles by the bucket-load. That's lucky for me because I always keep a few of these yuckity treats in my backpack. Here, pengy wengy!

Stunt Penguins can be found on the Frosty Pop Glacier, a wintry wonderland near Potion Ocean. When lost, they usually head for the nearest fridge.

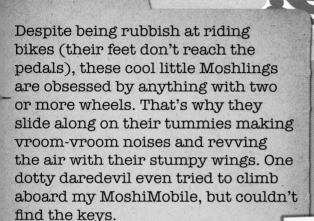

Habitat

Likes: ☺
Engine oil and buckets of fish heads.

Dislikes: ☹
Beards and being poked in the belly button.

Peekaboo!

Prof. Purplex
the Owl of Wiseness
074

Personality: bookish, well-read, well-fed

RARE

Prof. Purplex

Rockin' + readin'

Code to catch Prof. Purplex:

DRAGON FRUIT **ANY** + LOVE BERRIES **PINK** + MOON ORCHID **YELLOW**

Category: Birdies

Owls of Wiseness can be found high in the trees of Wobbly Woods. They don't like being disturbed and only leave the branches if they run out of reading/nibbling material.

Habitat

Banned by every library and bookshop in the land, Owls of Wiseness are brainier than big brain pies with extra brain sprinkles. Able to digest an entire encyclopedia in ten seconds, these birdie boffins have a real appetite for knowledge – literally, because they will scoff any book they see. That's why I always use my great uncle's old notebook as a trap – it's mighty interesting and covered in icky-sticky owl-grippy gloop. Now who's the brainy one?

Likes: ☺
Books, newspapers and plinky toy pianos.

Dislikes: ☹
Stupidity and bowler hats.

Meditating on his wiseness

Tiki
the Pilfering Toucan

Personality: mischievous, pesky, chirpy

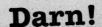
Scouting for shiny things . . .

Colourful but crafty, Pilfering Toucans can't resist 'borrowing' things from other Moshlings, especially salty gobstoppers. I say borrow, but what I really mean is steal, because these thieving flappers are the naughtiest pirates on the planet.

You won't believe how quickly they can swipe your pocket money and stash it in their beaks. Maybe it's because Pilfering Toucans once sailed the Seventy Seas alongside some of the meanest monsters in history. One thing is for sure, catching 'em is harder than knitting gravy. I always use a pile of gold coins and a big ol' net. Least I did – till they were stolen.

Darn!

Habitat

Pilfering Toucans nest high in the palm trees near Lush Lagoon. Look up and you'll see coconut-hair hammocks filled with all kinds of loot.

Likes: ☺
Playing the squeezebox and drinking punch.

Dislikes: ☹

Barbecues and catapults.

Watch out, Tiki's about!

Tiki

RARE

Code to catch Tiki:

STAR BLOSSOM		LOVE BERRIES		LOVE BERRIES
ANY	**+**	**PINK**	**+**	**RED**

Woolly

the Titchy-Tusked Mammoth

Personality: snuffly, old-fashioned, timid

Woolly

Habitat

Dozing in blocks of ice in ChillyBot State Park or eating hoodle plants around the Unknown Zone on Music Island.

Who says blue and green should never be seen? Not me because I know Titchy-Tusked Mammoths spend most evenings dyeing their pelts with Inka Inka essence and dipping their ears and feet in gloopy green puddles. These snuffly Moshlings are even said to be able to unscrew their tusks (which they sharpen using snooker cue chalk) and remove their woolly blue coats if it gets too warm. In fact, I still have a large collection of discarded titchy tusks (I found them, honest) on display in the loo at Bumblechops Manor.

ULTRA
RARE

Likes: ☺
Cotton candy kebabs and hairdryers.

Dislikes: ☹
Scissors and styling wax.

What weighs four tons and has sixteen wheels?
A Mammoth on rollerskates!

O'Really
the Unlucky Larrikin

Personality: luckless, optimistic, whimsical

If you're looking for a stroke of luck, best look away because Unlucky Larrikins are the most unfortunate Moshlings I've ever chanced upon. Not that they know it, because these upbeat critters are always looking on the bright side of life, whistling and joking, even when everything around them is going wrong. I used to travel everywhere with an Unlucky Larrikin (they were called Lucky Larrikins back then) but I soon grew tired of the bad luck and endless tall stories it insisted on telling me at bedtime. It must be the way they tell 'em.

Zzzzzz...

Near the fabled Barmy Stone of Shamrock Bog.

Habitat

144

RARE

O'Really

Likes: ☺
Limericks and rainbows.

Dislikes: ☹
Gold paint and
breakfast cereal.

Boomer
the Bigmouth Squiddly Dee

Personality: shrill, sensitive, volatile

Boomer

035

146

Stuff your ears with cotton wool because Bigmouth Squiddly Dees are seriously loud Moshlings. They might look all fluffy and harmless but every time you touch one it opens its gigantic cakehole and yells like a foghorn. But what's with the bandage? Well, I've recently discovered it's actually loo roll that they wrap around their fluffy heads to protect their ears from their own blaring shrieks. The trouble is this makes them a little hard of hearing. Indeed, I once snuck up on one and prodded it with my Moshiscope – bad move as it opened up and said

'Nyaaaaarghh!'

Eleventy Nook but I've spotted a few on Main Street. Yikes!

Habitat

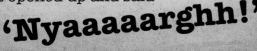

Likes: ☺
Soft loo roll and throat sweets.

Dislikes: ☹
Heavy metal and prodding.

Puppies

At first glance these cute little Moshlings seem just like regular doggies – happy and yappy with waggy tails and wet noses. But look a little closer and you'll see they are completely barking.

Yes, they love chewing bones and playing fetch. But they also enjoy dressing up as bouncy-wouncy frogs (Scamp), sipping vintage lemonade (Fifi), sniffing out secrets (McNulty) and tearing rubbish bins to bits (White Fang).

I've even seen a Puppy taking its owner for a walk!

Despite this oddball behaviour (well, they are Moshlings, after all) these mini-mutts make great pets. Just try to keep yours well away from any Kitties, or the fur will fly!

Oh yes, and don't be surprised if your seeds fail to flower when you're trying to attract a Puppy. Chances are, one of these frisky hounds will have dug 'em up and buried 'em in some other monster's backyard. You have been warned.

Woof!

Puppies are barking mad.

Fifi
the Oochie Poochie

007

Personality: swanky, fashionable, pushy

Fifi

Other Puppies:

McNutty the Undercover YapYap ✓

Scamp the Froggie Doggie ✓

White fang the Musky Husky ✓

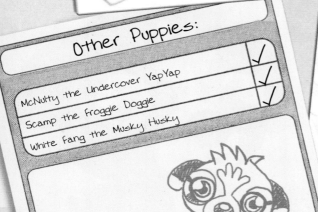

Likes: ☺
Ironed napkins and perfect manners.

Dislikes: ☹
A single hair out of place and being stroked.

Ooh la la! Oochie Poochies are sweet, fluffy and totally obsessed with the finer things in life, from fancy food to the very latest fur-styles. In fact, they love getting their fluffy bits trimmed and pampered. Whenever I observe Oochie Poochies they refuse to acknowledge me unless I've trimmed my whiskers and combed my fur. I even have to make an appointment to visit Uppity Meadow!

When they're not sipping vintage lemonade or collecting designer hair clips, these snooty little Moshlings like nibbling on the yummy cotton candy they keep on the end of their tails. Scrumptious, darling!

Paw print!

Fifi's got it licked!

Oochie Poochies adore the open spaces of Uppity Meadow, but some prefer parading around the Pink and fluffy forest.

Habitat

Code to catch Fifi:

HOT SILLY PEPPERS
ANY

+

DRAGON FRUIT
ANY

+

MAGIC BEANS
ANY

McNulty #038
the Undercover YapYap

Personality:
independent, loyal, furtive

McNulty

Code to catch McNulty:

STAR BLOSSOM		SNAP APPLE		SNAP APPLE
PURPLE	+	ANY	+	ANY

Psst . . . guess what?
Undercover YapYaps are the nosy puppies that love sniffing out secrets, rummaging through drawers and going 'psst'. With their plain fur and cuddlesome looks these cute snoops can dupe their way into any situation and are also masters of disguise. In fact, the only way to be sure you're dealing with one is to look out for that incredibly waggy tail. It's a dead giveaway! I used to get hoodwinked all the time, but not any more. These days I employ YapYaps to collect information for me. I'm even using my best snoop for a top secret mission.

Habitat

Undercover YapYaps often hang out in other Moshling neighbourhoods, but they originally hail from Sherlock Nook, south of Waggytail Hollow.

TOP SECRET

Likes: ☺
Gadgets, gizmos and trilby hats.

Dislikes: ☹
Wire coat hangers and muddy paw prints.

Scamp
the Froggie Doggie

Ribbit!

Personality: loopy-loo, deluded, hilarious

Pull here

Ribbit!

Ever wondered why a cute little puppy would want to boing around wearing a rubbery frog suit? Me too, but Froggie Doggies are too busy yelling 'ribbit' to answer silly questions. I keep several in my private zoo and I still can't work it out. Maybe there's something in the water? If you know different, feel free to get in touch.

Oh yes, and if you fancy catching one of these jolly pooches, just tug on its pink bow. It deflates that bizarre bouncy outfit in seconds. Ftsssst! If that doesn't work, try popping it with a pin. Bang!

Bang!!!!

Likes: ☺
Pond life and fairy princesses.

Dislikes: ☹
Garlic butter and knitting needles.

Code to catch Scamp:

DRAGON FRUIT	+	MOON ORCHID	+	SNAP APPLE
PINK		**BLUE**		**BLACK**

ULTRA RARE

Ribbit!

Ribbit!

Scamp

Habitat

Ribbit!

These dogs think they're frogs, so they often gather at Lillypad Lake and Croak Creek. Bad idea, as they can't swim. Ribbit!

White Fang
the Musky Husky
055

Personality: ravenous, slapdash, wild

Totally barking and slightly whiffy, Musky Huskies are the tail-chasing, bone-loving tearaways that will do almost anything for a bite to eat. I've even seen them rummaging through rubbish bins searching for scraps. Maybe that's why they always look so scruffy – why groom when you can scoff? Take care when stroking these greedy pups, or you might lose one of your delicious-looking fingers. Grrrrrr! At the start of a recent expedition a pack of Muskies nabbed my packed lunch. They even chomped my hooting honeybeans and nibbled my hiking stick. Thing is, I was still in my front garden!

Yummy bones!

Likes: ☺
Doggie bags and old bones.

Dislikes: ☹
Detangling lotion and getting tin cans stuck on their noses.

Code to catch White Fang:

MOON ORCHID

RED

+

MAGIC BEANS

RED

+

CRAZY DAISY

ANY

Because they're so hyper, Musky Huskies don't stay put for long. Check out a few skips and you might get lucky.

White Fang age 8 weeks

Habitat

White Fang [RARE]

Diary

Well tie me to an anthill and fill my ears with jam! Puppy Moshlings are almost as barking as I am! When they aren't woofing, whiffing, pawing and sniffing, these crazy little canines are usually seeking out monsters to take care of them. And that means they are dog-gone easy to catch, even without seeds or dogfood.

Why, just today I managed to bag myself two Musky Huskies, one Oochie Poochie and seven Froggie Doggies.

Woof woof!

The Huskies were simple. I just followed my nose to the nearest trash can and set a trap consisting of yucky leftovers and a big ol' bucket balanced on a stick. Poo, what a stink! (The Puppies, not the garbage.)

Trapping the Oochie Poochie was more of a challenge. These fancy bow-wows are highly educated, don't you know? I plonked a dinner table in Uppity Meadow and made sure the knives, forks and napkins were all messed up. I knew that any passing Poochies would be unable to resist tidying up — and I was right. The Oochie I nabbed even tried to fold the napkins into swans before my net fell. Oh, I say!

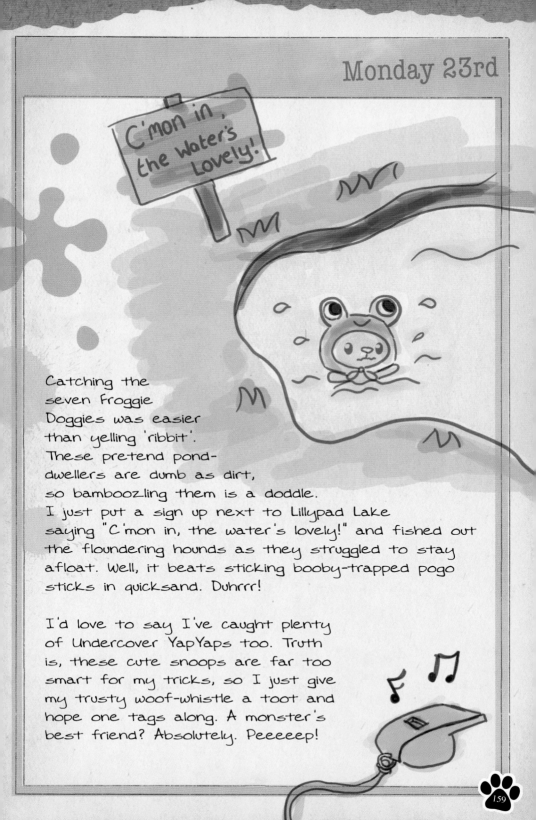

C'mon in, the water's Lovely!

Catching the seven Froggie Doggies was easier than yelling 'ribbit'. These pretend pond-dwellers are dumb as dirt, so bamboozling them is a doddle. I just put a sign up next to Lillypad Lake saying "C'mon in, the water's lovely!" and fished out the floundering hounds as they struggled to stay afloat. Well, it beats sticking booby-trapped pogo sticks in quicksand. Duhrrr!

I'd love to say I've caught plenty of Undercover YapYaps too. Truth is, these cute snoops are far too smart for my tricks, so I just give my trusty woof-whistle a toot and hope one tags along. A monster's best friend? Absolutely. Peeeeep!

Suey
the Bashful Bowlhead

#110

Personality: spicy, timid, popular

Suey

Habitat

Won Ton Bay on Hong Bong Island. You'll also find Bashful Bowlheads searching for fortune cookies in the Terry Aargh Keys.

Feeling peckish? Then why not hook up with a Bashful Bowlhead because these shy Moshlings produce a never-ending supply of slurp-tastic noodles from their bowl-like bonces. I first encountered a Bowlhead on Hong Bong Island. It was about to scarper so I grabbed it by the chopsticks before realising I needed a knife and fork. But then my translator, Dr Unwin Babble (who's travelled extensively in Hong Bong) explained that their chopsticks are actually sensitive feelers used to sense danger. It took me ages to get the soy sauce out of my socks!

Tasty!

Likes: ☺
Kittens of Good Fortune and five-spice flavoured crisps.

Dislikes: ☹
Cutlery and lemon dishwasher tablets.

What does Honey the Funny Bunny order at a Chinese restaurant? Hop Suey!

Betty

 # 037

the Yodelling MooMoo

Personality: ear-splitting, diva-ish, flirty

Betty

Habitat

Anywhere mountainous and snowy, from Sillimanjaro to their home village of StrudelHofen.

'Yodel-ay-hee-mooooo!' Next time you hear that unmistakable call you'll know that a Yodelling MooMoo is close by. But not that close because these opera-trained Moshlings can be heard from miles away. In fact, their yodelling is so loud I once asked a group of them to perform halfway up Mount Sillimanjaro – not because I enjoy yodelling; I just knew the racket would trigger an avalanche and clear my path to the summit. Unfortunately they insisted on joining me for the rest of the trip and yodelled the whole time. Worse still they brought along some Brassy BlowyThings and Squeezy Tinklehuffs.

Likes: ☺
Scoffing schnitzel and blowing the foam off Wobble-ade.

Dislikes: ☹
Jokes and dairy products.

Aargh!

Knock! Knock!
Who's there?
Moo
Moo Who?
No it's Moo Moo, not Moo Who!

Tiamo
the Sparkly SweetHeart

#032

Personality: delicate, benevolent, gracious

Tiamo

Habitat

I don't know for sure, but you can sometimes hear rhythmic d-dumfing near Blisskiss Valley.

Shhh . . . hear that? It's the gentle pulse of a Sparkly Sweetheart. These magical Moshlings often appear from nowhere to help monsters in distress with their sparkling energy auras. In fact, a Sparkly SweetHeart once saved my life when I was bitten by a hippopottimouth whilst searching for Oobla Doobla near the Bleurgh Lagoon. I've no idea what happened, I just remember hearing a faint d-dumfing noise and waking up, fully healed, surrounded by shimmering sparkles, a bunch of flowers and some grapes. Oh yes, I nearly forgot, when they are not performing life saving magic, Sparkly SweetHearts love d-dumfing to power ballads.

Likes: ☺ Power ballads and five bits of fruit a day.

Dislikes: ☹ Egg yolks and massage.

Dinos

Do you fancy having a totally Jurassic lark? Then why not bag yourself a few Dinos? These prehistoric Moshlings have been roaming the world of Moshi since the year dot. Maybe even longer.

Hatched from itty-bitty eggs, they are said to be descendants of a race of giant dinos (known as 'Doyathinkysaurus) but seem to have shrunk somewhere along the line. Either that or everything else just got a whole lot bigger.

As well as thick skin and a ridiculous fear of rubber spears and chest hair, Dinos have incredibly small brains. That's not to say they are dim, they are just a bit . . . erm, slow on the uptake.

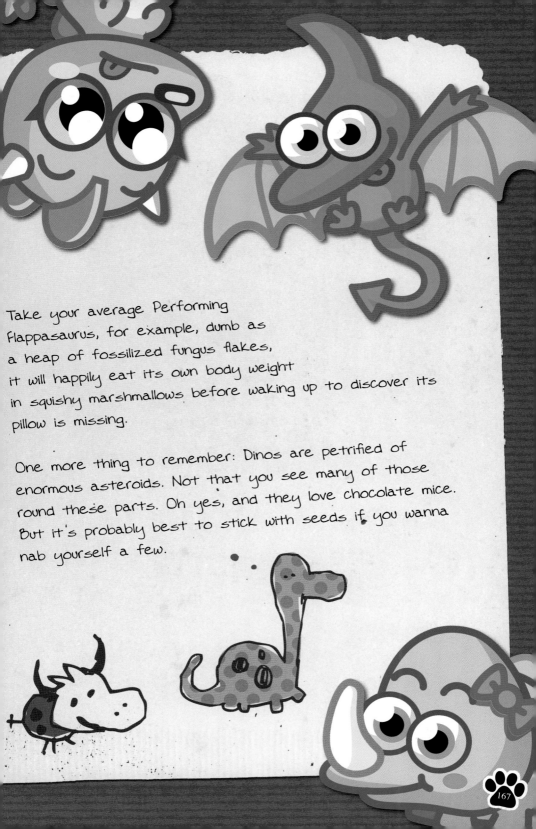

Take your average Performing
Flappasaurus, for example, dumb as
a heap of fossilized fungus flakes,
it will happily eat its own body weight
in squishy marshmallows before waking up to discover its
pillow is missing.

One more thing to remember: Dinos are petrified of
enormous asteroids. Not that you see many of those
round these parts. Oh yes, and they love chocolate mice.
But it's probably best to stick with seeds if you wanna
nab yourself a few.

Doris
the Rummaging Plotamus

Personality: gossipy, fluffle-loving, nosy

Doris

Other Dinos:

Gurgle the Performing Flappasaurus	✓
Pooky the Potty Pipsqueak	✓
Snookums the Baby Tumteedum	✓

Rummaging Plotamuses live anywhere there are fluffles to be found (usually under trees), so Friendly-Tree Woods is a popular hangout.

Habitat

Unlike regular Plotamuses, Rummaging Plotamuses are obsessed with digging for fluffles – valuable toadstools that smell of liquorice. These gentle Moshlings then knit the fluffles into nests and hibernate in them for much of the year. I was the first Moshi to tame a Rummaging Plotamus. I even got mine to knit me a fluffle jumper. Thing is, it smelt so good I couldn't resist munching it.

When they're not burrowing, knitting or snoozing, Plotamuses love gardening (well, digging up dirt) and gossiping about celebrities. And that's what makes them ideal pets – as long as you're not famous.

You dig?

Likes: ☺
Manicures and reading gossip columns.

Dislikes: ☹
Quiet Moshlings and tall garden fences.

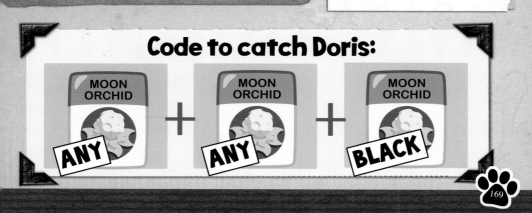

Code to catch Doris:

MOON ORCHID **ANY** + MOON ORCHID **ANY** + MOON ORCHID **BLACK**

Gurgle

the Performing Flappasaurus

Personality: prestidigitatory, fame-hungry, showy-offy

ULTRA RARE

Gurgle

Likes: ☺
Pulling rabbits out of hats and toasted marshmallows.

Dislikes: ☹
Bad audiences and soggy matches.

Habitat

170

What do you call a Dino with no eyes?
Do-you-think-he-saw-us?

Roll up, roll up! Performing Flappasauruses are the entertaining little Moshlings that always have a trick up their wings. The tricks usually go wrong, but I find it's best to applaud, because these jolly dinos are very sensitive. When a magic routine goes really badly I've seen them burst into tears and toast their props with a burst of fiery breath. But hey, that's showbiz! Examining Flappasauruses is pretty easy because they're massive show-offs. They'll even pose for photos and give interviews if you tell them you work for *The Daily Growl*.

Ta-daa!

Unlike most Moshlings, Performing Flappasauruses enjoy living in the full glare of the Cadabra Flash, a gleaming light formation near the Crazy Canyons.

Ta-daa!

Code to catch Gurgle:

DRAGON FRUIT — **RED** + LOVE BERRIES — **PURPLE** + MAGIC BEANS — **YELLOW**

Pooky
the Potty Pipsqueak

Personality: playful, imaginative, silly

Pooky

Code to catch Pooky:

MOON ORCHID **ANY** + MAGIC BEANS **ANY** + MAGIC BEANS **PURPLE**

How do Moshi Monsters like their eggs?

Terri-fried!

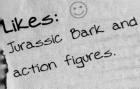

Likes: 🙂
Jurassic Bark and action figures.

Dislikes: 🙁
Washing their paws for dinner and sausage skins.

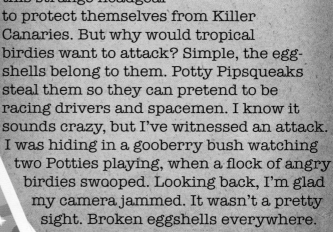

With their cracked eggshell helmets, Potty Pipsqueaks are often mistaken for newly hatched Moshlings. They claim to wear this strange headgear to protect themselves from Killer Canaries. But why would tropical birdies want to attack? Simple, the eggshells belong to them. Potty Pipsqueaks steal them so they can pretend to be racing drivers and spacemen. I know it sounds crazy, but I've witnessed an attack. I was hiding in a gooberry bush watching two Potties playing, when a flock of angry birdies swooped. Looking back, I'm glad my camera jammed. It wasn't a pretty sight. Broken eggshells everywhere.

Habitat

Potty Pipsqueaks come from Make-Believe Valley, but I've found them playing in cardboard boxes disguised as spaceships, fire engines and tanks.

Snookums
the Baby Tumteedum #010

Personality: timid, long in the tooth, trusting

Snookums

Habitat

If you find a yuckberry bush, you'll probably find a Baby Tumteedum lurking nearby. When they're not eating, these charming to gather near Stinky Holl

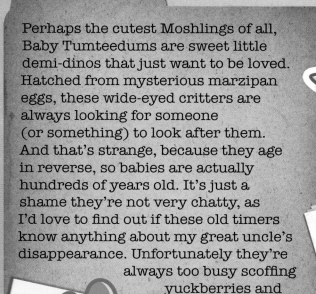

Perhaps the cutest Moshlings of all, Baby Tumteedums are sweet little demi-dinos that just want to be loved. Hatched from mysterious marzipan eggs, these wide-eyed critters are always looking for someone (or something) to look after them. And that's strange, because they age in reverse, so babies are actually hundreds of years old. It's just a shame they're not very chatty, as I'd love to find out if these old timers know anything about my great uncle's disappearance. Unfortunately they're always too busy scoffing yuckberries and boiled eggs dipped in vinegar.

Likes: ☺ Boiled cabbage and carpet slippers.

Dislikes: ☹ Loud music and toenail clippings.

Must remember to buy more vinegar . . .

Code to catch Snookums:

STAR BLOSSOM	STAR BLOSSOM	STAR BLOSSOM
ANY	ANY	ANY

Scarlet O'Haira

the Fluffy Snuggler

Personality: loving, cuddly, warm

Scarlet O'Haira

RARE

Frankly my dears, Fluffy Snugglers don't give a flying gooberry about silly ol' Moshling collectors like me. They're too busy snuggling each other. In fact, these happy little hairballs just adore hugging and love being loved, even if the thing they're hugging doesn't return the favour. I've seen Snugglers hugging lamp posts for hours on end. And I once woke up in my tent to find a few cosying up round my feet. Not that I'm complaining because they are incredibly warm. And with all that fluff it's hard to resist snuggling them back.

Mmmm, fluffy!

Likes: ☺
Hugging and pom-poms.

Dislikes: ☹
Frowns and naked flames.

Habitat

Lamp post lovers

You'd think being bright red would make Fluffy Snugglers easy to spot but I've yet to discover where they come from. Maybe I should just ask?

177

Oompah # 069
the Brassy BlowyThing

Personality: bright, boisterous, symphonic

Do you like parping? Good because these melodious Moshlings can't stop tooting thigh-slapping tunes whenever they smell sausages grilling or hear Wobble-ade fizzing. And that's why I've managed to collect so many of 'em over the years because I like nothing more than a few silly sausages washed down with Wobble-ade when I'm on an expedition. I've recently discovered that Brassy BlowyThings also enjoy burping rainbow-coloured bubbles when they march in time to their toot-tastic ditties.

Parp!

Likes: ☺
Lederhosen and Jolly Tubthumpers.

Dislikes: ☹
Kazoo solos and greasy fingers.

[RARE]

How do you fix a broken tuba?
With a tuba glue!

In Polka Park (alongside Squeezy Tinklehuffs) but some parp around Windypop Place.

Habitat

Oompah

Shambles #016
the Scrappy Chappy

Personality: happy-go-lucky, jumbly, plucky

Shambles

Happily hurtling through hedges

What a complete shambles! That's what most monsters say the first time they clap eyes on a Scrappy Chappy, because these hapless furballs look as if they've been dragged through a hedge backwards (and forwards and sideways and up and down). And that's not far from the truth because they enjoy the extremely dangerous sport of hedge diving. When they're not somersaulting into shrubbery you'll find them sitting high up in the trees nibbling their own ears. But don't worry, they grow back really quickly (and are absolutely delicious with a pucumber-based dip).

Wingledeed Woods but you'll need a ladder because Scrappy Chappies hang out on very high branches.

Habitat

Likes: ☺ Crumbs and ear-nibbling.

Dislikes: ☹ Styling wax and neckties.

Worldies

Introducing Worldies, the wacky Moshlings that bear an uncanny resemblance to landmarks you might just have seen somewhere before. Totally monu-mental, these walking, talking critters were once lifeless objects that sat hidden around the world of Moshi looking bored and neglected.

The poor things had been around for so long, most monsters didn't pay them much attention, unless they decided to pose beside one for touristy photos. In fact, the only creatures that visited Worldies on a regular basis were the birds - don't ask why, just use your imagination.

Plop!

But then one day, as if by magic, the Worldies suddenly came to life. It was as if they had been sleeping the whole time. Exactly how it happened is still a mystery, but I think it may have been caused by a blast of OoperDuper energy from deep inside the Umba Thunk Mines. Or maybe the Worldies just got bored with standing around all day.

Since waking from their slumber, Worldies have become extremely popular, especially amongst snap-happy sightseers and Moshling collectors. So read on and get planting . . .

Liberty

061

the Happy Statue

Personality: brash, confident, cheery

Liberty

Habitat

Likes: ☺
Big apples and star-spangled sweeties.

Dislikes: ☹
Rust and flash photography.

Happy Statues live on Divinity Island but rumour has it they were shipped over from a mysterious land called Prance.

With a lipsmackin' ice cream in one hand and a never-ending wish list in the other, Happy Statues believe in having fun, playing games and making wishes. They even wear magical crowns that glow every time they think up a new wish. It's not that these cheerful Moshlings are greedy, they just adore dreaming about yummy treats, cool clothes and twinkly trinkets. You go, girl!

Happy Statues are amongst my favourite Moshlings because they welcomed me with open arms (and lots of apple pie) when I first landed on Divinity Island. I wish all Moshlings were that friendly.

Pretty!

Liberty wishes it was raining jelly beans!

Liberty was designed by Moshling Collector Chaowzee in a design-a-Moshling competition!

Other Worldies:

Mini Ben the Teeny Tick Tock	✓
Cleo the Pretty Pyramid	✓
Rocky the Baby Blockhead	✓

Code to catch Liberty:

LOVE BERRIES **BLACK** + LOVE BERRIES **RED** + LOVE BERRIES **ANY**

Mini Ben
the Teeny TickTock

097

Personality: posh, dandified, eccentric

ULTRA
RARE

Mini Ben

Teeny TickTocks can often be spotted bonging around the foggy banks near Westmonster Abbey.

Habitat

Around the world

'CLONG!' Don't be alarmed, Teeny TickTocks are the noisy Moshlings who love chiming on the hour, every hour. I always stuff my socks in my ears when I'm tracking them down. Why? Because I once startled a sleeping TickTock and the bonging nearly burst my eardrums. Ouch!

When they're not swaying to and fro, making their bells go bong, these terribly old-fashioned chaps enjoy waxing their bushy moustaches, nibbling cucumber sandwiches and asking everyone the time. Well have you ever tried looking at a clock that's stuck on top of your head? It's harder than you think!

Likes: ☺
fish and chips with hot, sweet tea.

Dislikes: ☹
Earmuffs and cuckoos.

How can you tell if Mini Ben is hungry? He'll go back for seconds!

Code to catch Mini Ben:

SNAP APPLE	SNAP APPLE	SNAP APPLE
BLACK +	**BLACK** +	**BLACK**

Cleo
the Pretty Pyramid

080

Personality: sunny, smiley, fun-loving

What did one Pretty Pyramid ask the othe How's your mummy?

Most experts (but not me!) thought Pretty Pyramids were extinct, until a fierce sandstorm blew away a huge desert dune to reveal the lost valley where they live and play. Needless to say, yours truly was already on the scene following a tip-off. Thank goodness for that storm – I'd forgotten my shovel.

Apart from bathing in milk, munching on grapes and making massive sandcastles, these friendly Moshlings spend their days searching for lost treasure and painting funny squiggles on walls. They also love riddles, precious stones (especially Rox) and anything made of gold.

Likes: ☺
Their mummies and shiny, twinkly things.

Dislikes: ☹
Sandy suntan lotion and archaeologists.

Code to catch Cleo:

SNAP APPLE

YELLOW

+

CRAZY DAISY

BLUE

+

CRAZY DAISY

PINK

Habitat

Most Pretty Pyramids live in the Lost Valley of iSissi, near the banks of the River Smile.

Cleo

ULTRA RARE

Rocky

the Baby Blockhead

Personality: rugged, thoughtful, brave

Rocky

Code to catch Rocky:

HOT SILLY PEPPERS

ANY + LOVE BERRIES

ANY +

CRAZY DAISY

PINK

What is a Baby Blockhead's favourite music?
Rock and roll!

They might be stony-faced and a little dense, but Baby Blockheads can be really helpful. That's because these super-heavyweights are very, very strong – hardly surprising as they're made from solid rock! They even sweat liquid concrete when lifting heavy objects – bad news for me, as I once stood in a puddle of Blockhead sweat for a little too long and got stuck. Thank Moshi I only lost my boots!

Speaking of getting into trouble, Blockheads don't know their own strength and can sometimes break things, especially fingers when they're shaking hands. Crr-unch! Best to just say hi.

Let's ROCK!!

Likes: ☺
Rock music and fluffy rabbits.

Dislikes: ☹
Weeds and jackhammers.

Habitat

These incredible bulks live on Beaster Island where they often sit for hours, staring out to sea.

Diary

"Living thingies that look just like mini monster-made structures? You've gotta be kidding!" Yep, those were my exact words when I first heard about this bizarre band of Moshlings.

But then I stumbled across Rocky. Quite literally because the stony-faced statuette was hiding in the grass. Yow! Scared me silly and darn near broke my toe.

I soon discovered Blockheads are slower than treacle, so the next time I spotted one I dropped my hat on it and tried to pick it up. Big mistake, as these incredible bulks are amazingly heavy. Tore my hat, my undies and even a muscle in my back. If you haven't got the right seeds, I recommend you bend your knees when lifting one or buy a mighty big crane!

Much easier to catch are Happy Statues. I sometimes entice them with apple pie and twinkly trinkets, but they are usually happy to be nabbed by a living legend (that's me!) and simply follow me back home.

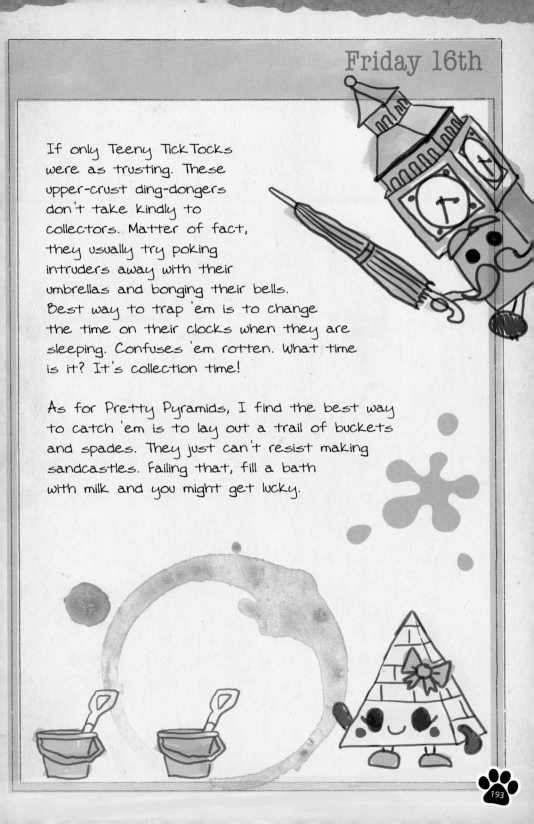

If only Teeny TickTocks were as trusting. These upper-crust ding-dongers don't take kindly to collectors. Matter of fact, they usually try poking intruders away with their umbrellas and bonging their bells. Best way to trap 'em is to change the time on their clocks when they are sleeping. Confuses 'em rotten. What time is it? It's collection time!

As for Pretty Pyramids, I find the best way to catch 'em is to lay out a trail of buckets and spades. They just can't resist making sandcastles. Failing that, fill a bath with milk and you might get lucky.

Penny

#011

the Mini Money

Personality: dithering, jolly, dizzy

Heads or tails? You choose because these lucky Moshlings love flipping themselves high up in the air, especially when they need to make important decisions. I used to be able to balance about fifty Mini Monies on my elbow and grab the entire pile with one hand when I was younger, but my reflexes aren't what they used to be. Nowadays I prefer to collect them and let them roam free around Piggy Bank Meadow on my Moshling Ranch. Rub one on its tummy and it might just bring you good luck.

Ker-ching!

Deep inside Dime Mine, but you'll sometimes see them flipping out on Windfall Way.

Habitat

Penny

Likes: ☺
Big pockets and metal detectors.

Dislikes: ☹
Falling down the side of the sofa and slot machines.

Scrumpy

the Surreal Snooper

Personality: nosy, surreal, officious

Say 'allo to the curious little Moshlings who just love solving mysteries, investigating strange goings-on and sticking their hyper-sensitive hooters into other Moshis' business. I once hired several Surreal Snoopers to look into the disappearance of my Great Uncle Furbert. What a waste of time that was! I soon discovered that these artful Moshlings really are surreal, when I caught one riding around my ranch on a pasta unicycle with a meat shoe on its head and a string of kippers round its waist.

Bonkers!

Habitat

Based in and around Strudel Station, but Surreal Snoopers like to nose around almost an_ area of the Moshi world.

Likes: ☺
The smell of oil paint and flash photography.

Dislikes: ☹
Pips and Ponies.

Scrumpy

How do you make an
apple turnover?
Push it down a hill.

Busling

the Bustling Busling

Personality: harried, stressed, regimented

The wheels on the bus go round and round? You bet they do because Bustling Buslings are the automated Moshlings who tootle around the world of Moshi, stopping every now and then to . . . erm, well they can't really pick up any passengers because they are a bit too titchy. Oh well, at least they enjoy themselves, dinging their dingers and trundling along in pairs. Stick out your arm and one might even pull over for a chat. But don't hold your breath – I've been waiting for ages now and my arm's really beginning to ache!

Habitat

Relaxing on little bricks in Blakey Hollow. Wait around on Main Street and two often show up at the same time.

Busling

The

EN GEN

Likes: ☺
Diesel-filled
doughnuts and
clear roads.

Dislikes: ☹
Lost property
and pushbikes.

Kitties

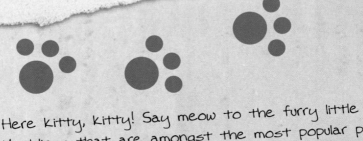

Here kitty, kitty! Say meow to the furry little Moshlings that are amongst the most popular pets in town. In fact, in tests, eight out of ten owners said they preferred collecting Kitties to almost any other Moshling. (The other two were too busy trying to catch Whinger Cats to comment.)

Aside from obvious stuff like paws, claws, teeth and tails, Kitties have several other things in common. Most of them enjoy lounging about, having their chins tickled and chasing balls of wool.

They hate hairballs too. Maybe that's why Furis often find collecting them a little tricky.

Rare Kitties such as Tabby Nerdicats are hard to entice, as they seldom leave home and find Moshling flowers a little boring. Actually, come to think of it, all four Kitties seem to prefer home comforts to the great outdoors.

This is probably because they want to avoid bumping into any Puppies. They're scared stiff of the yappy little pooches! In fact, the only time I've ever seen a Kitty scarper was when a Tubby Huggishi came face to face with a Musky Husky. It dashed back home to OuchiPoo Park before you could say

"Purrrrr".

Gingersnap
the Whinger Cat
003

Personality: sluggish, cantankerous, cynical

Gingersnap

Why is Gingersnap so whingy? He's always in a bad mewd!

Other Kitties:

Lady Meowford the Pretty Kitty

Purdy the Tubby Huggishi

Waldo the Tabby Nerdicat

☑
☑
☑

Grand gateau, yummy!

Moany, lazy, but strangely charming, Whinger Cats are said to be really good at fixing stuff. I'm not sure this is true, because they never bother showing up, even when I've ordered pizza for everyone. Maybe it's because they're busy waiting for other things – like bedtime and dinnertime. The first time I encountered one I mistook it for a cushion and sat on it. It didn't even flinch.

If you come across a Whinger don't expect it to move unless you've got a big handful of melted cheese – food is almost as important as sleep to these lovable layabouts. Yawn!

Paw Prints

Likes: ☺
All-inclusive hotels and melted anything.

Dislikes: ☹
Work, work and work.

Habitat

Whinger Cats are rarely seen outside as they spend most of their time chillaxing by Sloth Swamp near Hopeless Hill.

Code to catch Gingersnap:

HOT SILLY PEPPERS	LOVE BERRIES	MAGIC BEANS
ANY	ANY	ANY

Lady Meowford
the Pretty Kitty

030

Personality: snippy, sophisticated, snooty

Lady Meowford

Code to catch Lady Meowford:

STAR
BLOSSOM

ANY

+

MOON
ORCHID

ANY

+

MOON
ORCHID

BLUE

harp

Frightfully sweet but a bit annoying, these cute Moshlings are always right about everything. Well okay, there was one time when a Pretty Kitty thought it was wrong, but it turned out to be right all along. Snooty but impossibly charming, Pretties are very musical and have incredibly high-pitched singing voices. They also speak several languages, are very good skiers, fabulous lacrosse players and know everything about everything. I usually have to wear a tie and dinner jacket to get anywhere near one, and even then I can only speak when spoken to.

Likes: ☺
Classical music and toffee-nosed plums.

Dislikes: ☹
Balls of string and kebabs.

Habitat

Pretty Kitties live way up in the High and Mighty Mountains. Everywhere else is beneath them.

Purdy

020

the Tubby Huggishi

Personality: greedy, catty, lardy

Habitat

Tubby Huggishis are found all over OuchiPoo Park, usually in the sleepy valley near the Candy Cane Caverns.

Tubby Huggishis are highly huggable Moshlings that spend most days preening themselves and lounging about eating piles of pastry. That's why most of them are a little on the large side – good news for me as it makes 'em mighty easy to snag and tag. I've even had one eating fairy cakes from my hand. Big mistake as it darn near chewed my fingers clean off!

When they're not scoffing cakes, these shaggy felines enjoy giving advice to other Moshlings, dipping their paws in syrup and meowing to their friends about the price of lard.

Code to catch Purdy:

DRAGON FRUIT — ANY + MOON ORCHID — ANY + DRAGON FRUIT — ANY

Purdy

Likes: ☺
Drinking condensed milk
and licking stamps.

Dislikes: ☹
Water pistols and salad.

Waldo
the Tabby Nerdicat

077

Personality: dweebish, tech-savvy, inventive

Waldo

RARE

Code to catch Waldo:

DRAGON FRUIT

ANY

+

LOVE BERRIES

PINK

+

STAR BLOSSOM

RED

Category: Kitties

I thought I was geeky, but Tabby Nerdicats can tell you the square root of a banana faster than you can say "sci-fi convention". I even managed to persuade one to repair my camera after I dropped it in the bath – it makes the tea now, as well as taking photos!

Nerdis spend most days (and nights) fiddling with circuit boards, arguing over comics and listening to Quantum Physics Hour on Fangdoodle FM. Trying to find one is harder than reverse algebra, but I've discovered they like toffee nachos. Never ask 'em to dance. They can't.

Habitat

These studious Moshlings spend most of their time in cubbyholes by the grassy knoll on Honeycomb Hill. Do not disturb!

Likes: ☺
Untangling pretzels and fixing soldering irons.

Dislikes: ☹
Good dancers and contact lenses.

Techies

Reach for your toolkit and grab your spanners because Techies may contain nuts . . . and bolts, cogs, circuits, switches and screws. All of which is bad news for me because I'm a complete techno-dunce!

Truth is, you could write everything I know about technology on the back of a Mini Moshifone's sim card. So thank goodness Tamara Tesla says it's okay to call her with any tricky Techie questions (try saying that after a few Wobble-ades!).

Now all I need to do is learn how to use these new-fangled phones. Well, you try swiping and tapping with big furry mitts. Things were so much easier in the old days. A couple of swoonafish cans and a piece of string would do the trick.

Where was I? Oh yes, Techies. I'm not entirely sure how these mechanised Moshlings evolved into such handy critters but I'm sure glad they did 'cos they've bailed me out of several pickles. You just never know when you're going to need a Mini Moshifone to call for a Twirly Tiddlycopter to fetch a Happy Snappy to photograph a Titchy TrundleBot dragging you out of a pool of quicksand!

The only problem with Techies is that they are vulnerable to C.L.O.N.C. interference. Yes, really! Dr. Strangeglove and his contraption-savvy cronies are experts at reprogramming Techies to obey their mischievous orders. And I should know because a re-wired TrundleBot recently dug up all the goolip bulbs in my front garden!

Wurley
the Twirly Tiddlycopter

Personality: daring, noisy, naive

ULTRA RARE

Wurley

Habitat

Swarms of Tiddlycopters sometimes flitter over Nuttanbolt Lake but they spend most days hovering around Hangar Eight-and-a-Half.

Thanks to their motory-rotory headgear these tin-skinned flying Moshlings are always in demand, especially when they are transporting Rox and other precious thingies across the world of Moshi. As they wokka-wokka through the clouds, Tiddlycopters love humming classical music and performing loop-the-loops. I once asked a squadron of Twirlycopters to fly over the Gombala Gombala jungle to search for my long lost uncle, but all they could see was smoke pouring from a big bubbling cauldron. Psst . . . don't mention Dr. Strangeglove. He once tricked some Tiddlies into powering one of his diabolical glumping machines.

Other Techies:

Gabby the Mini Moshifone ✓

Nipper the Titchy TrundleBot ✓

Holga the Happy Snappy ✓

Likes: ☺

Windsocks dipped in oil (yummy) and cloudless skies.

Dislikes: ☹

Loose bolts and rain (it rusts the rivets in their tin flying jackets).

Holga
the Happy Snappy

Personality: nosy, chummy, flashy

Say cheese and strike a pose, because Happy Snappies are the Moshlings that just love taking photos, especially if there's a famous monster in town. Get the picture? You will, because they just can't resist handing out snaps to everyone they meet. I've often used Happy Snappies to help me photograph elusive Moshlings on my expeditions – risky as they have been known to run off and sell their pictures to Roary Scrawl at *The Daily Growl* in exchange for a few Rox!

Likes: ☺
Towering tripods and hot celebrities.

Dislikes: ☹
Lack of focus and shaky hands.

FLASH!

FLASH!

Holga

FLASH!

Habitat

Head to 35 Mil Hill, somewhere on Shutter Island, and you're sure to spot a few playing lens cap tiddlywinks.

Nipper
the Titchy TrundleBot

108

Personality: grabby, versatile, industrious

Need a hand? Better call a
Titchy TrundleBot! As well
as helping to build Monstro
City and clearing up the Great
Custard Flood of 99999.5, these
versatile Moshlings can pluck
Rox from the highest trees,
trundle across bumpy surfaces
and warn Monsters of falling
boulders. It's easy thanks
to their stretchy-flexi arms,
caterpillar-clad tootsies and
flashing hats. I even used a
few to help me out when I was
building Bumblechops Manor.
In fact, some TrundleBots
even know the location of my
secret ranch!

Habitat

TrundleBots love hanging
around construction sites but
are most at home playing
tag in Quivering Quarry.

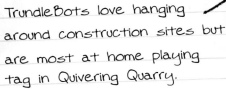

ULTRA RARE

Nipper

TOP SECRET

Likes: ☺
Stretching exercises and basketball.

Dislikes: ☹
Rusty wrenches and hardhats.

Gabby
the Mini Moshifone

Personality: chatty, tech-savvy, obliging

Gabby

Likes: ☺
Endless chit-chat and
18-month contracts.

Dislikes: ☹
Greasy mitts and
being dropped.

218

Mini Moshifones like to recharge in the electrifying atmosphere of the mysterious Voltage Vaults.

Whether they're flashing up funny messages, chatting to friends, playing games or composing new ringtones, these high-tech dinga-linging Moshlings are always on hand to help Monsters conduct long-distance chit-chats. My old friend

Habitat

Elder Furi has told me that they've even been used by Super Moshis on special missions because they are loaded with handy apps, including a Glumpass, a sicktionary and even a powerful laser. Just prod their fancy touchscreens and holler. It's for you-hoo!

Moshling Notes

Record the weird and wonderful ways you have added to your Moshling collection here. And don't forget to let ol' Buster know if you turn up anything extra special!

Moshling Notes

My Moshling

Personality:

Habitat

Likes: ☺

Dislikes: ☹

Category:

My Moshling

Personality: Dancing, Jiggli

Habitat

These moven Grovings love t. hang out at the party house.

These Jellys arent Just Tastey...... but yummy !!

Likes: ☺
Loud music and lights

Dislikes: ☹
darkness and party poppers

227

The Moshling Menace

Sigh, I remember the time when Moshlings could roam carefree around Monstro City with not a care in their itty-bitty brains. But times have changed. Not even Big Bad Bill is safe these days. My Moshling collecting is always done with the best intentions, but there are other shady characters out there who want to use Moshlings for far less friendly pursuits.

Yup, you guessed it, I'm talking about that dastardly Dr. Strangeglove! He's always finding new ways to round up the dinky little critters. If he had his way, all the Moshlings in Monstro City would be turned into Glumps to do his devious deeds!

So, watch out fellow collectors, as you never know where Strangeglove or his minions might turn up next

WANTED

FOR DOZENS OF DASTARDLY DEEDS

DR. STRANGEGLOVE

My Photos

Photographing flipping
fishies frolicking for fun

230

My Photos

I had a ranch full of very hungry Moshlings the day Elmore the Great fell and blocked the grub truck from reaching Monstro City!

The Daily

CAPTURED!

Breaking news! Roxy the Precious Prism, has finally been caught by Moshling Collector Extraordinaire, Buster Bumblechops! Buster told *The Daily Growl* that he'd been digging up mutant sprouts in his allotment when a glistening glint in the distance caught his eye.

Catching Roxy shouldn't be so tricky for the rest of us! Buster is willing to share his secret with readers of *The Daily Growl* and help all Ultimate Moshling Collectors to get their hands on this priceless prize. Simply email Buster at **buster@moshimonsters.com** to find out more . . .

Above: Roxy the Precious

On Tour!

The Moshi MonStars have just announced their new tour! Tickets go on sale at noon tomorrow and the queues already stretch all the way down Main Street to The Port!

Above: The Moshi MonStars

Above: Elder Furi

Growl

All the ooze that's fit to print!

Strangeglove Spotted!

Moshling collectors beware! Dr. Strangeglove has been sighted sneaking around Monstro City in search of Moshlings to Glump in his increasingly incredible Glumping machines! No Moshling is safe while Strangeglove is at large. Please contact the Super Moshis with any information on his location.

Inside today's *Daily Growl*:

- Ruby Scribblez interviews Zack Binspin!
- Best buys at the Bizarre Bazaar
- En-Gen Roarkers strike!

ew Recruits Needed!

o you think you ave what it takes to olve crimes, take art in monstrous nissions and wear our pants over your rousers? Then the

Super Moshis need you to help protect Monstro City! Head down to the Volcano and look for Elder Furi to sign up now!

Tyra's Spa

Win a fabulous monster makeover at Tyra's Spa with our competition. Turn to page 26 for details on how to enter!

lucy's moshlings

Burnie
#78

Humphrey
#23

Jeepers
#73

ULTRA RARE!
ShiShi
#87

ULTRA RARE!
Zack Binspin
#107

Roxy
#101

ULTRA RARE!
Pocito
#111

Angel
#24

ULTRA RARE!
Gigi
#79

Mr. Snoodle
#56

Priscilla
#48

ULTRA RARE!
Leo
#98

ULTRA RARE!
Bobby SingSong
#112

Rofl
#29

Coolio
#52

ULTRA RARE!
Cutie Pie
#91

Hansel
#59

ULTRA RARE!
Oddie
#88

ULTRA RARE!
Plinky
#106

ULTRA RARE!
Blingo
#103

Cherry Bomb
#75

MOSHLING ZOO

hop Chop
#02

General Fuzuki
#82
ULTRA RARE!

Sooki-Yaki
#47

Shelby
#39

Wallop
#05

Shelly
#12

Jessie
#99
ULTRA RARE!

Dipsy
#34

Flumpy
#54

Honey
#57

IGGY
#100
ULTRA RARE!

Rooby
#62

Gracie
#15

Fizzy
#76

Blurp
#43

Cali
#72

Fumble
#53

Stanley
#18

Pip
#09

Judder
#14

Tingaling
#63

Big Bad Bill
#89

Ecto
#60

Kissy
#27

Squidge
#08

HipHop
#36

Tomba
#66

CocoLoco
#109

DJ Quack
#13

Peppy
#71

Prof. Purplex
#74

Tiki
#65

Woolly
#58

O'Really
#70

Boomer
#35

Fifi
#07

McNulty
#38

Scamp
#84

White Fang
#55

Suey
#110

Betty
#37

Tiamo
#32

ULTRA RARE!

238

Doris
#40

Gurgle
#83

Pooky
#50

Snookums
#10

Scarlet O'Haira
#67

Oompah
#69

Shambles
#16

Liberty
#61

Mini Ben
#97

Cleo
#80

Rocky
#28

Penny
#11

Scrumpy
#41

Busling
#04

Gingersnap
#03

Lady Meowford
#30

Purdy
#20

Waldo
#77

Wurley
#105

Holga
#45

Nipper
#108

Gabby
#25

Buster's Lost Moshlings App

Help Buster find his lost Moshlings with this app from Moshi Monsters!